An Exceptional Friendship

THE CORRESPONDENCE OF
THOMAS MANN AND
ERICH KAHLER

An Exceptional Friendship

THE CORRESPONDENCE OF THOMAS MANN AND ERICH KAHLER

Translated from the German by
Richard *and* Clara Winston

Cornell University Press | ITHACA AND LONDON

Cornell University Press gratefully acknowledges a grant from the Andrew J. Mellon Foundation that aided in bringing this book to publication.

177656

First published 1975 by Cornell University Press.
Published in the United Kingdom by Cornell University Press Ltd., 2-4 Brook Street, London WıY ıAA.

International Standard Book Number 0-8014-0830-X
Library of Congress Catalog Card Number 73-20794

Printed in the United States of America by Cayuga Press, Inc.

Contents

Translators' Preface

Erich Kahler — or von Kahler, as he was known until, in American exile, he chose to drop the prefix of nobility — met Thomas Mann in 1930 or 1931. At the time Thomas Mann was already world-famous as the author of *Buddenbrooks, Death in Venice,* and *The Magic Mountain.* Some of his greatest work still lay before him, but he had already received the Nobel Prize for Literature (1929). Erich Kahler, ten years younger than Mann, had published comparatively little. But his *Das Geschlecht Habsburg* (1919) had received high praise from Hugo von Hofmannsthal and Stefan George. And his *Der Beruf der Wissenschaft* (1920), a reply to Max Weber's *Die Wissenschaft als Beruf* (1919), had started a lively discussion in Germany and gained Kahler the reputation of being one of the important thinkers of the German-speaking world. Although he devoted himself chiefly to historical and philosophical writing, he associated with the somewhat *précieux* devotees of pure form in the Stefan George circle. Friedrich Gundolf and Karl Wolfskehl were among his friends.

Emil Preetorius, the artist and stage designer, may have introduced Kahler to Mann; but in the intense, almost familial atmosphere of literary and artistic Munich, introductions were hardly necessary. Everyone in the circles devoted to *Geist* and *Kunst* knew everyone else. Acquaintance ripened into friendship when the two men shared exile in Zurich after 1933, and into intimacy from 1938 to 1941 in Princeton, where the Kahler home at One Evelyn Place was only a short walk and an instant telephone call from Stockhaldi, as the Manns called their house at 65 Stockton Street.

Erich Kahler, who adapted rapidly to America and acquired a remarkable command of English, often took the lead in interpreting American conditions to Mann. Kahler's preoccupation in his historical studies with the evolution of human consciousness made him one of the foremost interpreters of Mann's fiction — which in turn exemplified and helped to shape some of Kahler's theories. Kahler wrote most of his major books in America, and in English. He managed to do so while earning a living by teaching, and while generously devoting much time to helping his friends, among them the novelist Hermann Broch, who lived in his house for many years and who relied heavily upon Kahler's critical acumen. Midway in age between the older and the younger generation, Kahler became the friend and confidant of the Mann children. His warm relationship with them and with Thomas Mann's wife, Katia, continued after Mann's death in 1955, until his own death in 1970.

The present volume contains all the extant letters exchanged between Thomas Mann and Erich Kahler. Unfortunately, many of Kahler's replies to Mann are missing; the Manns moved many times after 1933, and letters went astray because of the vicissitudes of exile. The core of the present volume is a translation of *Thomas Mann–Erich von Kahler: Briefwechsel im Exil,* edited by Hans Wysling, the distinguished director of the Thomas Mann Archives in Zurich. This correspondence was published in Zurich in 1970 as Number 10 of the Blätter der Thomas Mann Gesellschaft. To that core the translators have added letters omitted from the *Briefwechsel im Exil* but included in Thomas Mann's *Briefe,* edited by Erika Mann and published in three volumes by S. Fischer Verlag (Frankfurt, 1961-1965). In addition, all available unpublished letters have been translated.

The translator of correspondence must strive to keep separate the voices with which he is dealing. In the present case the voices are so distinct, and the translators have had so much experience working with each separately, that they feel confident of having overcome this difficulty. One insoluble problem remains: the subtle shading of salutations. "Dear" and "My dear" scarcely convey the elaborate courtesies and circumspection implied by "Lieber und verehrter Freund" as compared to "Lieber, verehrter Freund" and "Lieber, Verehrter." Lacking the conventions, we in the English-speaking world may also lack a sense of the delights and embarrassments to which those conventions give rise. We must accept the loss. The reader of a translation is always slightly impoverished, and when the writers are stylists like Thomas Mann and Erich Kahler, the impoverishment can be considerable. The translator does what he can.

Grateful acknowledgment is made to The Caroline Newton Thomas Mann Collection in the Princeton University Library for providing copies of Thomas Mann letters that have not hitherto been published; to Margaret E. Aschaffenburg for deciphering and typing some of those letters; to the Thomas Mann Archives, Zurich, for copies of Erich Kahler letters and several of Thomas Mann's letters; to the Thomas Mann Gesellschaft, Zurich, for permission to translate *Thomas Mann– Erich von Kahler: Briefwechsel im Exil;* to Katia Mann for permission to use the letters of Thomas Mann and one of her own; and to Alice Kahler, Erich Kahler's widow, for permission to use Kahler's letters and for locating two drafts of letters among his papers. She has also contributed, in ways too numerous to mention, to the completion of this project. It remains, finally, for us to thank William A. Koshland of

Alfred A. Knopf, Inc., and Thomas Rosenthal of Martin Secker & Warburg Limited for permission to use our own translations of seventeen Mann letters previously published in *Letters of Thomas Mann, 1889-1955,* copyright © 1970 by Alfred A. Knopf, Inc.

Marion Kaplan, of Cornell University Press, prepared most of the notes. The first note of each letter indicates the provenance of the letter.

In Erika Mann's edition of the *Briefe,* certain passages were omitted, usually to avoid repetition, occasionally for reasons of discretion. In the present book, such passages have been restored. Wherever three dots appear, they are simply punctuation marks used by the writers. All the letters by Mann and Kahler are published without deletions except for one instance in which a few words of scribbled postscript have been omitted to avoid giving offense to a living person. For the same reason, one name has been disguised.

RICHARD AND CLARA WINSTON

Halifax, Vermont

About Erich Kahler (1885–1970)

Erich Kahler was born in Prague in 1885. When he was fifteen, his family moved to Vienna, and it was there that he began his studies of history and philosophy. He pursued these at the universities of Berlin, Munich, and Heidelberg. In his student years he formed ties with other young men later to be prominent as members of the Stefan George circle. Eventually he returned to Vienna, where he received his doctorate. In 1912 he married and established himself in Wolfratshausen, near Munich, which remained his home for the next twenty years.

At the time of the fateful election in 1933, Kahler and his wife were visiting his mother in Vienna. Although he crossed back into Germany in order to cast his vote against the National Socialists, some instinct warned him not to return to his home. In fact, ten days after the election and the Hitler victory, the Gestapo raided the Kahler house. They were particularly intent on confiscating the manuscript of Kahler's major work at the time, a survey of German history which Kahler had already submitted for publication. This later appeared in Zurich under the title *Der Deutsche Charakter in der Geschichte Europas* (1937). Later, writing in English, he drastically rewrote this book, and the English version has recently been published as *The Germans* (Princeton, 1974).

For the next five years the Kahlers lived in Switzerland, where the friendship with Thomas Mann, also in exile there, ripened further. In October 1938, the Kahlers emigrated to the United States and settled in Princeton. The year 1941 marked a significant caesura in Kahler's career. His marriage of thirty years had come to an end, and his life was henceforth linked with that of Alice (Lili) Loewy, who was to remain his companion until the end. In 1969 they were married. Kahler also embarked on a vigorous round of teaching, lecturing first at the New School for Social Research and then assuming duties at other universities in the United States and abroad. From 1947 to 1955 he was professor of German literature at Cornell, and from 1960 to 1963 at Princeton. In 1949 he became a visiting member of the Institute for Advanced Study at Princeton. He was Lord Simon Fellow at the University of Manchester in 1955-1956, Merschon Fellow at Ohio State University in 1959, guest lecturer at the Munich Technische Hochschule in 1963-1964, and a member of the Deutsche Akademie für Sprache und Dichtung. In 1967 he presented the Faber Lectures at Princeton, which in 1969 awarded him an honorary degree.

Kahler was the author of numerous articles in American, Austrian, German, and Swiss periodicals, essay collections, and anthologies. Some of his books were published only in German, some only in English, others in both languages. The titles of the books published in English indicate the wide range of his interests: *Man the Measure: A New Approach to History* (1943); *The Tower and the Abyss: An Inquiry into the Transformation of Man* (1957); *The Meaning of History* (1964); *The Jews among the Nations* (1967); *Out of the Labyrinth: Essays in Clarification* (1967); *The Disintegration of Form in the Arts* (1968); *The Orbit of Thomas Mann* (1969); *The Inward Turn of Narrative* (1973); and *The Germans* (1974).

An Exceptional Friendship

THE CORRESPONDENCE OF
THOMAS MANN AND
ERICH KAHLER

Kahler to Mann

Wolfrathshausen im Isartal, [Germany]
March 13, 1931[1]

My dear Herr Thomas Mann:

Preetorius[2] has already transmitted our invitation for you to spend a few days out here with us. Along with that I want to make a somewhat unusual request. I feel I should explain my motives rather carefully, so as to offer at least some justification for this request.

Years ago, very nearly five years now, I became involved in a project whose subject and tendency, if they are to be propperly dealt with, call for a new approach to the work[3] and a new form. Impelled by the psychic and political distress I have seen all around me, I wanted to undertake an elemental rethinking of the essence of Germanism. I don't mean a "German History" or a "Psychology of the German," but a graphic summary of what we can call specifically German, what we can define as the German racial character. I did not want to analyze and psychologize academically, to line up single traits, let alone construct a system consisting of isolated traits. That has been done so often and seems to me utterly useless for practical purposes. Instead I wanted to show the organically rounded, morphic coherence of a character to the mind's eye with the same kind of vividness with which the keen physical eye can instantaneously grasp the form or features of a person. Thus I wanted to apply to a people's racial character, to a breed of men with a specific psychology, a method friends have applied to great individuals

[3]

in books that have by now become famous and are well known to you. It is the method I myself tried on a family in my book *Das Geschlecht Habsburg* ["The House of Habsburg"].[4]

Faced with the dimensions of a national character, with the completely unique strata of Germanness, this endeavor of mine is confronted with entirely new and peculiar problems of form. If I had decided to depict the French character, say, or the English, I would at any rate have been able to give an ordered picture, for there we have fixed, finished, decided characters. But with Germanness what is involved is a still fluid type, one which has not yet reached its specific character, which is still in the process of becoming. If, therefore, it is to be grasped as an organic whole, it must be excavated from its historical conditions and supplemented by imaginary possibilities. This dynamic folk cannot be represented in terms of its potential traits. Thus it is necessary to write "history," but a special kind of physiognomic history: the history of the evolution of the German character. To complicate the matter further, there is the universality of this German character, so that the history of the human race is involuntarily contained in this evolutionary account, and its beacon light must be made to blaze as well. This is all the more essential today, when all concepts have become wavering and iridescent, when we can no longer assume a single historical concept as absolutely given and established by convention, when each concept to which we refer must instead have been elaborated, in fact newly created, from its own special conditions. When we talk about feudalism, capitalism, state, monarchy, etc., we must explain beforehand exactly what we mean by these terms in relation to this folk. We must explain the special meaning of each word so thoroughly and simply that any man of good will who is prepared to listen, any "ideal illiterate," so to speak, will be able to absorb the picture without needing all kinds of preliminary knowledge. In short, we

[4]

must at one and the same time write philosophical and funda-mental history. So you can see what problems of form loom up in the course of this confounded, not to say presumptuous undertaking: to fix visually something that is in dynamic flux; to define specifically something involved with universals — to do all this with accessible conceptual elements, and all this in such a way that the construct can be grasped by an un-biased human mind through the medium of a humanly com-mon language.[5]

Alongside the special problem of form runs a special problem of publication. For years my closest friends — Gundolf, Preetorious, Wolfskehl,[6] and others — have been urging me to publish those portions of the work that have been completed. Each of them knows only parts of it, and cannot have the entire architecture of the book in mind as I do. My own sense of the times is also urging me, my feeling that I ought to meet and may possibly miss the demands of the hour. A task conceived on so large and long-term a scale is in grave danger of being undermined by its own times. Finally, a natural impatience and desire to have some effect upon the world are also urging me. Of course, this impulse is one I ought least of all to yield to, and on this point, at any rate, I think I am certainly in the right. On the other hand, I am the only one who knows what shape the finished work is meant to have, and all that still has to be added so that what has already been developed will stand in its rightful place and its importance be seen. In this case above all, where everything depends on the timeless, perfectly coherent and cogent relationship of all individual aspects, it torments me to think of exposing to public view a torn fragment in which nothing but a hundred started threads seem to be hanging in the air.

Still and all, I recently arrived at a point at which I could at least consider the possibility that what has been done so far is a section in itself, a relatively independent complete thought; that it has attained a degree of preliminary coherence, so that the outlines can be sensed and I can therefore venture to begin with the publication. There are many arguments against that procedure and some for it. In order to separate the objective from the subjective factors, I am impelled to appeal to the advice and the artistic conscience of a man who combines human impartiality and receptivity with what is so exceedingly rare in Germany: productive knowledge of the secrets of form. You will spare my expatiating on why I have placed my hope in you. Granted, I cannot say what entitles me to make such a claim upon your time when I venture to ask you to listen to me read, or to look over by yourself, the entire section that has been completed so far. Only the success or failure of my work can decide whether this claim is a purely personal matter or whether it can to a degree be justified on the grounds of the work's general importance. Right now the request is sustained by nothing but a simple human confidence in your frequently proved readiness to be helpful where the things of the mind are concerned.

Yours,
Erich von Kahler

1. From a draft found by Alice Kahler among her husband's papers.

2. Emil Preetorius (b. 1883), president of the Bavarian Academy of Fine Arts in Munich, stage designer, artist, writer, book designer, collector of Asiatic art. He was responsible for epoch-making reforms in the presentation of Wagner's operas.

3. *Der Deutsche Charakter in der Geschichte Europas* ("The German Character in the History of Europe" [Zurich, 1937]; *The Germans* [Princeton, 1974]).

4. Munich, 1919.

5. Erich Kahler's use of "human" and "humanity" has certain peculiarities which he later defined as follows in his *Man the Measure: A New Approach to History* (New York, 1943): "To speak

of a feature of the human being as humanity may appear to be a tautology. But it is not a tautology, because the species man, and so mankind, unfortunately cannot be identified with the behavior we call humanity. This behavior is an exclusively human feature, but it is not a general feature of mankind."

6. Friedrich Gundolf (1880-1931) was a leading German literary critic. Karl Wolfskehl (1869-1948), writer, in 1938 emigrated from Italy to New Zealand; his *An die Deutschen* is among the great poems of exile literature. Both were members of the Stefan George circle. Stefan George (1868-1933) was the leader of the revolt against realism in German literature and of the Symbolist school of poetry in Germany.

Mann to Kahler

Munich
March 18, 1931[1]

My dear Herr von Kahler:

Your letter honors me and has given me great pleasure. What you have to say about your work, and the invitation you extend, so fascinate and move me that I am more than ever ashamed of the objections I raised in my conversation with Preetorius, in which I spoke of how overburdened I am with work and how severely subject to fatigue. But what's to be done? These factors remain and I must rationally take them into account, even if a momentary indisposition were not depressing me and specially reminding me of them. That will pass, but my general situation remains: this concern for a many-layered, problematical, refractory task, alongside of which run a hundred other affairs and trivialities — the result of a perhaps too conscientious compliance with the desires and demands of the world. In any case I feel myself painfully in arrears with those matters. "Trials," says Goethe, "increase with the years." Since we make them for ourselves, we are allowed to be proud of them; but the trouble is that in the purely athletic sense we ourselves are not always in top form when they reach the top of their curve. Although at first we find it extremely unwonted and repugnant, given a certain ready willingness of character, we must "learn to conserve our strength." A disagreeable, insipid, and disconcerting phrase, but one day it simply becomes more than just an empty phrase; it becomes an expression of the need to know what we want. On the 25th I am going to Berlin for the celebration of my brother's sixtieth birthday.[2] This is a matter of both emotion and honor. I must speak in the name of the Prussian Academy and participate in other formal affairs. All this was arranged long ago. It will cost me four or five days, not including the preparation and aftermath. In May a trip to Paris is impending for a lecture long since agreed to out of God knows what sense of duty. I would certainly have read your letter poorly if I thought these obligations more important than the visit to Wolfratshausen and a joint reading of your work in days that could well be a wonderful festival of friendship and ideas. I am aware of the important bearing this work has on mine, and I am truly grateful that you yourself have considered it. But those other commitments do happen to be older and I cannot, without falling into conflict with myself, add to them new undertakings, absences, irregularities, and festivities. It may sound ridiculously boastful, but I have responded to five or six such temptations with plain refusals before exercising the severest self-discipline of all and saying no to you too, as I must.

I am not being vain when I say that you would have found me a good listener. So much the worse. My consolation is that I shall not be any less attentive a reader. I should like to be one soon; but this is not the only reason that I venture to advise: Give the times their due and publish what you have written. I understand your inhibitions, but we believe

[8]

until almost at the end that the decisive word remains to be written, and yet we have always set down far more of the decisive words than we ourselves can possibly appreciate. Go into print and permit us to read! I can think of no more important gift to us Germans than the book your letter describes to me, and I have no doubt that the first volume alone will be such a gift.

Sincerely yours,
Thomas Mann

1. *Letters of Thomas Mann, 1889-1955,* trans. Richard and Clara Winston (New York, 1971); copyright © 1970 by Alfred A. Knopf, Inc.; hereafter cited as *Letters.*

2. Heinrich Mann (1871-1950), Thomas Mann's elder brother, the author of many novels, from 1931 to 1933 was president of the section for fiction of the Prussian Academy of Arts in Berlin. In 1933 he emigrated to southern France; in 1940 he escaped to the United States and lived in California near Thomas Mann.

Mann to Kahler

Küsnacht-Zurich
March 19, 1935[1]

Dear Herr von Kahler:

I read your proofs to the end day before yesterday and am fascinated to the depths of my soul. The book[2] is far and away the most elevating and penetrating thing I have seen on these problems. Reading it, in fact, I had the feeling that it is precisely your characteristic fusion of Judaism with Georgian Germanism, and no other combination existing today, which establishes your right and vocation to speak validly on all this — and by "all this" I mean not only the German-Jewish question, but also the problem of Europe itself. The extended chapter on Germanism and Judaism is incontestably the truest and the phychologically keenest statement ever made on the subject — and I say that as a German with an overseas Latin admixture[3] who in the course of time has grown more and more disgruntled with living among Germans, and who cannot wholly forgive certain generous extenuations in your estimate of them. I felt closest to you in the passages which arouse a kind of tragic cheerfulness, such as the one about "vain knowledge" of the inevitable disillusionment of a "mighty faith." In a few truly poetic lines, you make us feel the painfulness of such a symbiosis: on the one hand, the ironic mother wit of old cosmopolitan blood, and on the other hand, the credulity of a crude psyche bound to the flesh.

I hope the book does come out at last — it almost doesn't matter where any more. Is there any chance at all for it in Germany now, after the recent threats to the Jewish publishing houses? On the other hand, I well understand that it is intended for Germany, even written with a great deal of concern for Germany, and perhaps it could come out there. But what do we really know about the situation? And what Swiss or Dutch publisher would not be delighted?

After this, there is scarcely need for my little memorandum.[4] Would you just mail the text back to me, printed matter, sometime?

I hope we shall be seeing you soon. Regards to you and your wife.

Thomas Mann

1. *Letters.*

2. *Israel unter den Völkern.* Completed at the end of 1932, it was destroyed several times by the Nazis while being set. It was finally published, in Zurich, in 1936. (*The Jews among the Nations* [New York, 1967] is not a translation or revision but an entirely different work).

3. Thomas Mann's mother, Julia da Silva Bruhns Mann (1851-

1923), was born in Rio de Janeiro of a Brazilian mother and a German father.

4. An opinion that Thomas Mann had written for Bermann Fischer on *Israel unter den Völkern*. In view of the political situation, the memorandum had become unnecessary. Gottfried Bermann Fischer (b. 1897), physician and publisher, in 1934 had become head of the venerable publishing firm of S. Fischer Verlag, which he moved to Vienna, then, after the *Anschluss,* to Stockholm. Expelled from Sweden in 1940 for anti-Nazi activity, he moved to the United States, where he helped found L. B. Fischer Corp. In 1950 he re-established the firm of S. Fischer Verlag in Frankfurt and Berlin.

Kahler to Mann

March 21, 1935[1]

Dear Herr Thomas Mann:

Thank you from the bottom of my heart for the great pleasure you have given me by your approval, by your cordial reception of this book. I have become so uncertain about the impression it makes nowadays, because except for the recently revised final section, it was written some three years ago, in Germany and for Germany, and at the time was intended to bring about a pause for reflection on both sides. But now it is already too late for that by an immeasurable span of time. I am beyond it; events have gone beyond it . . . Nevertheless, it represents an accounting of a situation already lived through, and the premise for everything I should have to say about these matters, and which I feel the most insistent urge to say. Today I could not create this basis for a second time. Therefore I was anxious to learn whether the book might still have some objective validity. Since the question of publication is coming up once more, I shall take its meeting the standards of the noblest reader, though

[11]

also a most benevolent one, as proof that it may after all stand up even under present conditions.

Beyond that, it also took care of my need to communicate with you. It was a feeble means of thanking you for your magnificently angry speech,[2] which uplifts heart and mind. I wanted to let you know how much this resounding accord means to me. May I confess to you that in the boundless misery of this present-day world there is indescribable comfort in the intellectual and human closeness to you and the pleasure of sometimes conversing with you.

All good wishes to you and your wife.

Yours,
Erich Kahler

P.S. I shall send the speech back tomorrow. Could it somehow be arranged for me to have the proof sheets for a time? Perhaps we could meet sometime in town.

Incidentally, Dr. Philipp Löwenfeld[3] requested me yesterday to ask you for your brother's address; he has to get in touch with him.

1. Thomas Mann Archives, Zurich.

2. *Achtung, Europa!* (Stockholm, 1938; "Europe, Beware!" in *Order of the Day: Political Essays and Speeches of Two Decades,* trans. H. T. Lowe-Porter, A. E. Meyer, and E. Sutton [New York, 1942]).

3. Dr. Philipp Löwenfeld, Kahler's lawyer in Munich, who fled to Zurich (with only a toothbrush in his pocket); he was also Kahler's lawyer later in New York.

Mann to Kahler

On board
Cunard White Star *Berengaria*
July 11, 1935[1]

Dear Herr von Kahler:

With memories of your handsome birthday salute,[2] which I did not have the chance to read on the outbound voyage and which was and will remain a great pleasure, I do want to send you and your wife a traveler's greetings from our return voyage.

We have many varied impressions behind us. At the awarding of the doctorates to Einstein and me at Harvard[3] the audience of five thousand converted the ceremony into an impressive demonstration by a mighty ovation, and in Washington we had a very interesting dinner at the White House with President Roosevelt. The meeting has greatly reinforced my bias in favor of this man.

We'll be seeing you soon. Tomorrow we depart from Cherbourg directly for Zurich.

Yours,
Thomas Mann

1. The Caroline Newton Thomas Mann Collection in the Princeton University Library; hereafter cited as Princeton.

2. Thomas Mann's sixtieth birthday was June 6, 1935. His American publisher, Alfred Knopf, had invited Mann and his wife, Katia, to visit the United States in June. Mann, who had exiled himself from Nazi Germany and was living in Switzerland, was greeted in America by testimonial dinners and receptions, and gave numerous talks and interviews.

3. Mann received an honorary Doctor of Letters degree.

Mann to Kahler

September 6, 1935[1]

Dear Herr von Kahler:

Vita Nova had already sent me a carbon of your letter. I told the publisher I was sorry about his decision but thanked him for the intelligent and humane tone of his rejection. It is, though, rather tactless of him to want you to take a more religious rather than a mythic approach.

So what now? It is as if the book[2] were bewitched, and yet one is reluctant to abandon the faith that the world must welcome what is good and useful. I am expecting Bermann to visit in the next few days. If it turns out that he will be leaving Germany (which I keenly hope and which I shall strongly urge him to do), he is the logical publisher for the book. So I should like to wait until we've spoken before venturing any further advice; the fruitlessness of my previous advice has shamed me. Meanwhile you will have looked into the question of how the Vita Nova Verlag means its offer of help and counsel. If need be, we might have to revert to the Humanitas publishing house after all. For my part, I would prefer not to see the book published by an explicitly Jewish house. It is by no means solely for Jews, and nowadays Jewish publishers don't have many non-Jews among their audiences.

Good wishes. *Auf Wiedersehen.*

Yours,
Thomas Mann

1. Princeton.
2. *Israel unter den Völkern.*

[14]

Mann to Kahler

Küsnacht
February 1, 1936[1]

Dear Herr von Kahler:

Would you mind sending me the proofs? I need them after all.

I have just written a possibly memorable letter to the *N.Z.Z.*[2] It has completely preoccupied me these past several days, so I did not get around to thanking you for your card and Brentano[3] for his letter. But tell him that Father Kesser[4] did not greet us in the Nord-Süd Cinema yesterday; he was so ostentatious about not recognizing us that it was a bit thick. What solidarity with his sonny boy — against whom I have done nothing, either.

Yours,
Thomas Mann

1. A postcard; Princeton.
2. In response to an article by Eduard Korrodi, "German Literature in the Exile's Mirror," *Neue Zürcher Zeitung,* January 26, 1936, Mann wrote a letter to Korrodi, dated February 3, which was published as an open letter by the *Neue Zürcher Zeitung.* The letter points out that all writers exiled from Nazi Germany were not Jews and asserts that the German rulers' hatred of the Jews was directed not only against the Jews but "against Europe and all loftier Germanism" and "against the Christian and classical foundations of Western morality." The letter led directly to Mann's "expatriation" by the Nazi authorities.
3. Bernhard von Brentano (1901-1964), a novelist and essayist who emigrated to Switzerland.
4. Hermann Kesser, whose son Armin had written a review of Heinrich Mann's *Die Jugend des Königs Henri Quatre (Young Henry of Navarre)* for the *Neue Zürcher Zeitung.* Displeased with the review, Thomas Mann had written Eduard Korrodi, the newspaper's feature editor, that he did not wish to see Armin, who had been friendly with Thomas Mann's son Klaus, again.

Mann to Kahler

Ragaz, [Switzerland]
June 16, 1937[1]

Dear Herr von Kahler:

Cordial thanks for your efforts! In heaven's name, it never occurred to me that my letters to Klaus[2] which I mentioned to Lion[3] were to be included in the first issue. In fact, inclusion of the letters to Lion in this issue seems to me *de trop* after the foreword and the chapter from the novel.[4] All I meant to do was to show my support for Lion's idea of a gossipy insider's column. I find this idea really attractive, but I promptly added that finding suitable material for it would probably be no less difficult than finding major articles for the main section.

The letters to Klaus are not even accessible. I have no idea where they are, and from that fact alone you can see that my suggestion was hardly meant concretely. But please tell Oprecht[5] to write Lion that I should also not like to have the letters addressed to him in the first issue. They can come along in some later issue, but I would stress that they should not be published by themselves, but always covered and framed by other things of a similar nature.

My doctor here wisely prepared me for the painful reaction that was to be expected.[6] He was absolutely right, and I have had difficult days and nasty nights. It is no fun at all for my poor wife. And two weeks must pass before we can hope for improvement. Then, after the first effects of the thermal baths are over, the electrical Stanger baths begin. I cannot even think of receiving visitors yet. You, my dear Kahler, would be just the right person, but anyone in addition would be bad for me. I have no staying power, and everything tires me excessively. Let us see how things are going in another ten days, and then arrange something.

Hearty congratulations on the completion of your work. Many regards from both of us.

Yours,
Thomas Mann

1. Princeton.

2. Thomas Mann's son Klaus (1906-1949), a prolific novelist and journalist. He edited the magazines *Die Sammlung* in Amsterdam and *Decision* in New York. During World War II he served in the American army.

3. Ferdinand Lion (1883-1965), an Alsatian essayist and cultural critic.

4. Thomas Mann was a founder of the journal *Mass und Wert* (September 1937–November 1940), which published the work of émigré writers. Mann was editor-in-chief. Ferdinand Lion was for a time managing editor. To the first issue Mann contributed a foreword and a chapter from *Lotte in Weimar* (1939; *The Beloved Returns*, 1940).

5. Emil Oprecht (1895-1952), a Swiss bookseller who went into publishing because of a deeply felt opposition to Hitler, founded Europa Verlag, which published *Mass und Wert*.

6. Mann was in Ragaz to take treatments for sciatica.

Mann to Kahler

Jamestown, R.I.
May 26, 1938[1]

Dear Erich von Kahler:

Tomorrow, Friday, Erika[2] will be in Paris, and at the beginning of next week in Zurich. She will bring you and other friends our greetings and our tidings. But I don't want to leave it entirely up to her; I want to tell you myself how often we think of you, and with how much sadness, and how acutely we will miss you in our future life. You do understand our decision, don't you? We very much hope and wish that people in Zurich and in Prague will also understand it. The shock of the crime against Austria was severe; the parallel with 1933[3] forced itself upon us; we felt it as a "seizure of power" on the continental scale, and again we had the sensation of being cut off, as in 1933. All this may prove to be exaggerated or premature. Nevertheless we cannot regret our decision and our act of "immigration"; there are too many good reasons, in Europe and here, for making this country our residence at least for a time, although we shall keep in touch with the old continent as much as possible. The reception of *Joseph in Egypt*[4] here, and my tour from East to West and back again (which, in spite of all the strains connected with it, might have been a merry harvest festival had it not been for the anxieties and alarms over Europe), have shown me how much trust, sympathy, and friendship are given us here. And how can I help feeling attracted by this atmosphere of warmth and friendliness, when these are so totally lacking in Europe. I also believe that more and more of the better "Europe" will be moving here, including German publishing, so perhaps the German editions of my books may even appear here. In short, it seems to me that my place is here now. The thought that by leaving Europe at this point we shall very possibly escape the war is actually of secondary importance. My reason cannot believe in the war. No one wants it or can possibly want it, because of the unforseeable consequences. But on the other hand, reason also tells me that nothing but war can be the result of what is brewing in Europe now.

Our little country to the east[5] is behaving wonderfully. I prefer not to express the feelings that the behavior of the Germans arouses in me.

After the wanderings of the past three months, we have come to a temporary resting place here at the seaside in a borrowed cottage, and I am taking up the thread of *Lotte in*

Weimar as I would have done in Küsnacht. For the autumn I am making an arrangement with Princeton for a kind of honorary professorship which will not impose an excessive burden upon me and will provide a basic livelihood. We will therefore settle there around September. The place has the advantage of being rural, with very good connections to New York.

And what about you? And your mother? What plans do you have? Or rather, what wishes? Naturally I was thinking of you when I said that the better Europe will gradually be moving over here to join "us." *Auf Wiedersehen!* Here or in Switzerland, where we shall almost certainly be coming on a visit soon — perhaps as soon as next winter.

Yours,

Thomas Mann

1. *Letters.*

2. Thomas Mann's daughter Erika (1905-1969) was an actress, journalist, and the author of several books. Her father relied on her for editorial and practical advice.

3. In March 1938, following the invasion of Austria by German troops, Austria was incorporated into the German Reich (*Anschluss*). In 1933, the Nazis had seized control of the major centers of power in the German government and enabled Hitler to rule by decree.

4. Volume III of Thomas Mann's *Joseph and His Brothers*. The four volumes are *Joseph and His Brothers, Young Joseph, Joseph in Egypt,* and *Joseph the Provider.*

5. Czechoslovakia.

Mann to Kahler

65 Stockton Street
Princeton, N.J.
October 19, 1938[1]

Dear Kahler:

I would gladly have written to you long ago — I have thought of you so often during these weeks, felt anxious about you and yours, and wished that I could talk with you about the common misfortunes. But you can imagine how I have been living: first the disturbing days of uncertainty in Paris, then the week of depression along with the painfully inadequate news aboard ship, then the hours of tense hope after arrival here, culminating in a gigantic mass meeting in Madison Square Garden, at which I spoke and witnessed tremendous demonstrations; then Munich, and the realization at last of the filthy play which was being performed all along. The denouement came when the "democratic" governments transmitted Hitler's blackmail threats of war to their own people. . . . The shame, the disgust, the shattering of all hopes. For days I was literally sick at heart, and in these circumstances we had to install ourselves here. Now I am over the worst of it, have accepted the facts, whose meaning and logic is only too despicably clear. And now, I am tempted to think by magic, my desk stands in my study with every item arranged on it exactly as in Küsnacht, and even in Munich. I am determined to continue my life and work with maximum persistence, exactly as I have always done, unaltered by events which injure me but cannot humiliate me or turn me from my purposes. The way that history has taken has been so filthy, such a carrion-strewn path of lies and baseness, that no one need be ashamed of refusing to travel along it, even if it should lead to goals we might commend if reached by other paths. But who knows what further atrocities this trail may still pass through? Yet that Hitler will die as a transfigured prince of peace and chancellor of a fascistic United States of Europe remains improbable.

I have made similar remarks in a preface to the small collection of political essays[2] that Bermann[3] meant to publish (whether he still wants to and can, I do not know). I felt the need to bring these outmoded things up to date, so the essay is also called "Up to Date." I like the title. But whether anything of the sort can still be printed in Europe is now extremely doubtful. People here are already highly suspicious of all European sources of information and believe that the censorship is widening. Naturally the peoples of Europe must not be allowed to realize too quickly how they are being hood-winked and bullied.

I read a few lines of yours, a letter to Lion that he sent to me. The happiest news I gathered from it was your growing resolution to come over here. Do so! What's the sense of staying now? And how fine it would be to live as neighbors. Our house, which belongs to an Englishman, is very comfortable and an improvement over all those of the past. I think it important always to fall upstairs. The people are well-meaning through and through, filled with what seems to me an unshakable affability. You would breathe easier among them, would be touched and happy. The landscape is parklike, well suited to walks, with amazingly beautiful trees which now, in Indian summer, glow in the most magnificent colors. At night, to be sure, we already hear the leaves trickling down like rain, but people say that the clear, serene autumn often continues until nearly Christmas, and the winter is short.

The youngest children are with us. Erika is arriving tomorrow, probably with Golo,[4] whose Czech military obligation doubtless need no longer be a problem, thanks to Chamberlain's[5] deep love of peace. Erika was in Prague.... I am curious to see what kind of European atmosphere the children will bring with them.

With friendly regards,

Yours,

Thomas Mann

1. *Letters.*
2. *Achtung, Europa!*
3. Gottfried Bermann Fischer.
4. Golo (Gottfried) Mann (b. 1909), Mann's second son, was a historian who taught in France. He later was coeditor of *Mass und Wert.* In 1940 he emigrated to the United States, where he taught at several universities. He has been a prolific writer on historical subjects; his major work is *Wallenstein* (Frankfurt, 1971).
5. Arthur Neville Chamberlain (1869-1940), the British prime minister whose policy of appeasement of Hitler and Mussolini led to the Munich Pact (1938), which permitted Hitler to annex the Sudetenland to Germany without interference by France and England. In return, Hitler promised he would make no further territorial demands in Europe.

Mann to Kahler

Le Havre

June 13, 1939[1]

Dear friend Kahler:

So — Europe. Very well, let's see what comes next. We could not have wished for a finer crossing than we had. Your travel blessings worked — many thanks for them! We have decided to proceed from Paris to Holland first, Nordwijk: mailing address Querido [Verlag]. It will be better to *postpone* Switzerland. We wish you a pleasant summer. I must hope for a quiet atmosphere for work at our destination.

Cordially yours,

T. M.

Warmest regards and more soon!

Yours, Katia M.[2] & Erika

1. A postcard; Princeton.
2. Katia Pringsheim Mann (b. 1883), the wife of Thomas Mann, was the daughter of Alfred Pringsheim, a professor of mathematics, and had been a student of mathematics and physics.

Mann to Kahler

Noordwijk aan Zee
June 28, 1939[1]

Dear Friend:

It is really time that our thoughts of you and wondering how you are were set on paper. I would gladly have written long ago, but this climate is extremely strenuous, at once disturbing and tiring, and limits capacity for work to a modest minimum. At least that is how it affected me in the over-strained condition in which I arrived here, and it is something of a misfortune that circumstances prevented us from going to Switzerland at once. Such strong climatic medicine as this should have come after rather than before. The thing is that the gangsters have made a contract with my father-in-law, arranging for his majolica collection[2] to be auctioned off in London — ostensibly in his name. He must appoint the representative of the Ministry of Economics as his agent. The Reich government will receive 80% of the proceeds in foreign currency; the remaining 20% will be left abroad for him,

[23]

and he is to receive a passport to go abroad as soon as the payment is made. The first auction has taken place — with moderately good results. The second is to follow on July 19 and 20. In any case, we have been asked not to show our faces in Switzerland until the old folks have their passports, with which they will, I hope, go straight to the airport from the police station without returning home, where probably somebody will already be waiting to take the passports away again on behalf of some other bureau. Perhaps the passports won't be forthcoming at all, in spite of the gangster contract, and we are being foolish. God forgive me, but I gnash my teeth somewhat about all this.

At the same time this waiting posture has such great advantages that one might almost regard it as an end in itself. A magnificent ocean and an excellent hotel — I have always appreciated the combination of starkness and comfort. But naturally there is a great deal of wind, and the weather is still remarkably cold, and the sixty-four-year-old organism is resisting adjustment to new demands, after it has just protested its adjustment to American conditions by an outbreak of shingles.

As far as work goes, I've finished off a trifle in my beach chair: the foreword for the new edition [1939] of *Royal Highness,* which Knopf insisted on. But I'm already running into serious hitches with the introduction to *Anna Karenina* [1939] that I have now begun working on, even though — after a rereading — everything I had to say was really quite ready. Yesterday I was reminded of *Lotte* when I read aloud from some of the earlier parts to my brother-in-law Peter and his wife,[3] who have been here on a three-day visit with us. I suppose I shall be doing the dinner scene once the mumbling[4] is over; but I am still rather in the dark about the end, and I often wish that clever elves would finish the book overnight. When we were parting, you seemed to have some kind of advice or a warning in regard to the mumbling on the tip of your tongue. Please don't keep it back, whichever it was, when you write! I can use it.

After America, Europe with its military customs officials and passport scrutinizers seems narrow, overcrowded, and ill-tempered. At least it did as long as we were traveling. We obtained the Belgian transit visa only through a letter of recommendation from the Dutch ambassador in Paris, but then it entitled us to expedited treatment and great respect at borders. I am, alas, profoundly reassured, much too reassured, about our getting away from this continent with a whole skin. I don't even believe that thoroughly fascist Europe has the slightest desire to wage this war, *our* war. Its outcome would be certain — which is all the more reason for it not to take place. To my feeling, some horrible appeasement is hanging in the air instead. Chamberlain's most recent speech was once again full of the basest treachery. Right on top of it came Roosevelt's grave defeat in the Senate[5] — doesn't that give us a lift!

Let us hear how you are and where you are. News that Frau Fine[6] has gained a few pounds would do a great deal to cheer us. My wife and Erika send warm regards. All of us are looking forward to seeing you in the fall.

Yours,
Thomas Mann

1. *Thomas Mann–Erich von Kahler*: *Briefwechsel im Exil,* ed. Hans Wysling, Blätter der Thomas Mann Gesellschaft, No. 10 (Zurich, 1970); hereafter referred to as *Briefwechsel.*

2. Alfred Pringsheim's collection of Renaissance majolicas was world famous. See O. von Falke, *Die Majolika-Sammlung Alfred Prings-heim in München* (2 vols.; Leiden, 1914).

3. Peter Pringsheim (1881-1963), Katia Mann's brother, a professor of physics in Brussels after 1933, fled to the United States in 1940. His wife, Emilia (née Clément), was Belgian.

4. Chapter vii of *Lotte in Weimar,* containing Goethe's monologue.

5. Roosevelt attempted to remove from the existing Neutrality Act the mandate that the President put an embargo on the export of munitions in the event of war.

6. Erich Kahler's first wife.

Kahler to Mann

Woodstock, N.Y.
August 6, 1939[1]

My dear Friend:

I have a very guilty conscience because I am so late in answering your welcome letter. I received it in sweltering New York, where I was working with a translator trying to make a big essay for *Social Research*[2] as English as possible, and at the same time as much my English as possible. This collaboration has proved to be the right way to establish a direct and variegated connection between English and me; I learn a great deal in the process, and fortunately I have at last found an excellent translator — I work very well with her. But since this had to be done on some of New York's hottest days, it was quite strenuous.

The result was that I did not arrive here, where it is lovely and half European, until the last week in July. This Woodstock is really in a ludicrous way an American version of Ascona [Switzerland]. The village center is less attractive, of course. It is the well-known "street," somewhat more crooked than main streets usually are and if possible even more temporary and trumpery — a row of sheds in which the shops, the post office, various inns, diners, and summer dancing places are housed. There are also an art exhibition and a playhouse. But all around, in the hills and in the woods, painters, musicians, writers, and so on live in very handsome studios. Fairly near our cottage, on our own Byrdcliffe hill, there is the Villetta, a veritable Monte Verità, a hotel for intellectuals, with a kind of Schwabing tradition,[3] which was built by one of the legendary founders of the whole Woodstock colony and today, after his death, still belongs to his heirs. In an adjacent building there are a remarkably fine neglected international library and a lecture hall where Byrdcliffe Afternoons are held: series of lectures and discussions on a given theme under the aegis of several professors from Columbia and Chicago who have long had their summer houses here. In the first series Slochower[4] was one of the speakers (on Dos Passos and Steinbeck). He also talked quite a bit about you — in general, during the discussions on art you hovered over the minds here in a way that made me feel very much at home. The second series is a more political one, arranged by the American Association for the League of Nations, i.e., the institute for intellectual cooperation. It deals with Latin America and is somewhat more instructive for me. A man from the State Department in Washington spoke about the history of Central America, which I know very little about, and next time the former Spanish ambassador (for the Loyalists), de los Ríos,[5] will talk. But the principal thing is still, as always in such cases, sociable pleasure in elevated chatter, which continues in cocktail parties. In Europe all such affairs were a horror to me, of course, but here people are so much more childlike, eager, receptive, and unconstrained that I sometimes am glad to take part in such events, and even Fine does occasionally.

But what is lovelier and rarer is the countryside here, which is something basically new to me. Beneath echoes of the Wienerwald, the Salzkammergut, and England, and beneath a deceptive sweetness, an utterly alien and limitless wildness repeatedly bursts forth, and the beautiful, far-ranging woodland strolls that are possible here all end unexpectedly on the brink of jungle-like impenetrability. There is a mountain that

[27]

is scarcely a thousand meters high, and it even has an effort-less road leading up to it, since somebody tried to build a hotel up there, but it remained unfinished and is now said to form a grotesque modern ruin — we are planning to climb up there soon, but must actually be prepared to meet a bear or a rattlesnake; both are by no means rare. Animal life altogether is unusually plentiful and varied. There are wonderful birds and butterflies, a charming intermediate form between rat and squirrel (chipmunk); and the tremen-dous din produced at night by the different varieties of cicadas and tree crickets puts your powers of sleep under a considerable strain. You understand the Americans better when you experience nature as it is here (and here it certainly reveals itself in its mildest and most civilized form). These people live only on the periphery of their country; they have mastered neither the breadth nor the depth of it. And they have something of this nature in themselves; they have like-wise failed to master their own depths. Just like this enor-mous country, they have covered themselves with a thin rational layer of civilization and haven't yet become aware of their own fundamental irrationality and inner wildness. Strangely enough, it is easier to establish an affinity with such qualities in nature than in man. I think this would not be a bad region for you, if you make up your mind some day to try an American summer. If one rents one of these hand-some and cozy houses in the woods, near the splendid high-ways, one has at any rate a perfect "combination of starkness and comfort."

I hope that in the interval you have overcome the some-what irritable state of mind your letter expressed and have found your way back to work and to real recuperation, inso-far as it is still possible in Europe. I wonder where you are — in Sweden or in Switzerland after all? Do come back in good time — the autumn offers an uneasy prospect. Although I can no more imagine a war than you can, some unpredictable explosive upset is all too likely. Things certainly cannot go on the way they have been going.

I am looking forward to the continuation and possibly even the conclusion of *Lotte;* perhaps those elves that work inside you have after all found the right ending. As for the mumbling, my thoughts about that were by no means such that they should have exerted any influence whatsoever upon it. They were observations on the relationship between your own nature and Goethe's, on the hiding places and underground corridors that you have so cunningly found for highly personal statements — on this whole deep combination in which the lovely obscurity of the work of art is and must be preserved in the teeth of talent, inclination, and plan. So these remarks were intended more for myself than for you and were only a manifestation of conscience.

My plans for work on a larger scale have been coming back to me here — if only the world would leave a bit of psychic space for that sort of thing! One must train oneself to plan and work under this atmospheric pressure as if the anarchy of these times did not count. But first comes an essay for *Mass und Wert* that I have promised Golo — on democracy![6]

Thank God, Fine is feeling somewhat better here. She has gained back six of the twenty pounds she lost, and is calmer, gayer, and more sociable. She sends her warm regards.

Please don't be annoyed and let me hear from you again before fall: where and how you are and how everything has gone. Since no member of the family is in the vicinity, we are completely cut off from communication.

Warmest good wishes and remembrances until we see you again, which I hope will be soon!

Yours,
E. K.

1. *Briefwechsel.*

2. Erich von Kahler, "Forms and Features of Anti-Judaism," *Social Research,* 6 (November 1939).

3. Monte Verità is in Ascona, Switzerland. Schwabing is the artists' quarter of Munich.

4. Harry Slochower (b. 1900), American literary critic and psychoanalyst, is the author of many books, including *Thomas Mann's Joseph Story* (1938) and *Mythopoesis: Mythic Patterns in the Literary Classics* (1970).

5. Fernando de los Ríos (1879-1948), who helped to overthrow the Spanish monarchy, was ambassador in Washington, 1938-1939, for the republican regime. After Franco's victory he joined the faculty of the New School for Social Research.

6. Erich von Kahler, "Was soll werden?" *Mass und Wert,* 3 (March–April 1940), 300-322.

Mann to Kahler

February 22, 1940[1]

Dear Friends:

The next-to-last station of our Calvary. Interesting! Spanish baroque in sky blue and dust — a special kind of southland, full of character, beautiful Mexican people. A good many shabby tricks have been played on us. Soon we will be back with you to complain.

>Yours,
>Katia and Thomas Mann

1. A postcard from San Antonio, Texas (Mann was on a lecture tour in the Southwest); Princeton.

Mann to Kahler

441 North Rockingham
Los Angeles-Brentwood
July 8, 1940[1]

Dear Friend:

I feel the need to say how much we wish that we had you here together with us during this period of agonizing and numbing expectation. It is painful and constricting that we should be so far apart now of all times. The hour of decision is almost upon us, and there is little hope that the brainless fanatics will not succeed in attaining their every end. The world and the times show a distinct disposition to let them succeed, perhaps not only out of weakness and affinity to evil, but also out of the instinct to view these desperate fanatics, who nevertheless have a talent for victory, as an instrument for still unknown but necessary aims and purposes. The situation is ghastly, a torture to the mind and the emotions. Everything depends on England's capacity for resistance, which no one can estimate. If she falls in one way or another, the gates are thrown open to hell itself *everywhere*. We must prepare to face total defenselessness and homelessness, with eternity the only refuge. I have always believed that maintaining a kind of personal serenity can bring one safely through the darkest circumstances, and I have trusted to my capacity for adaptation. But these days I often feel hopelessly trapped.

We have had a few days in Mount Kisco [New York] — very pleasant outwardly, although somewhat too sociable; but then again that helped to distract the mind. The Busch quartet was there together with Serkin[2], and I heard for the first time a most magnificent quintet of Brahms, more like a symphony than chamber music — something to remember. The trip here was swift and comfortable, with a single day's stopover with the Borgeses[3] in Chicago. We have moved into a rather magnificent roomy house in a hilly landscape strikingly similar to Tuscany. I have what I wanted — the light; the dry, always refreshing warmth; the spaciousness compared with Princeton; the holm oak, eucalyptus, cedar, and palm vegetation; the walks by the ocean, which we can reach by car in a few minutes. There are some good friends here, first of all the Walters and Franks,[4] besides our two eldest children [Erika and Klaus], and life might be enjoyable were it not that our spirits are too oppressed for pleasure — and for work also, as I discovered after some initial attempts. We know nothing about my brother, nothing about my wife's brother, nothing about Golo.[5] For the latter, diplomatic inquiries are in progress; San Domenico and Brazil, whose ambassadors we have had the good fortune to make friends of at Mount Kisco, are both trying. But the success of these efforts remains dubious. Erika has been called to England, and is capable of throwing herself into the turmoil there. At least she intends to wait another month.

Our warm regards to you and your wife and mother. Katia, too, means to write to you. Medi laughed herself to tears over the hermit. "Why, he's so terribly sensual!" she cried again and again. She notices everything, you know.

Yours,

Thomas Mann

1. *Letters;* date from postmark.

2. The Busch Quartet was founded by the violinist Adolf Busch (1891-1952), who emigrated to the United States in 1942. Rudolf Serkin (b. 1903, Czechoslovakia), the concert pianist, is a cofounder of the Marlboro Music Festival.

3. The writer and scholar Giuseppe Antonio Borgese (1882-1952), who lived in the United States after 1931, was married to Thomas Mann's daughter Elisabeth (Medi). On the way to Princeton from Los Angeles, Katia and Thomas Mann stayed for a while with their son-in-law's family in Chicago.

[32]

4. Bruno Walter (1876-1962), the conductor, had become a close friend of Mann while the Manns were living in Munich, where Walter was general director of musical activities, 1912-1922, In later years he was a neighbor of the Manns in California. Bruno Frank (1887-1945), poet, novelist, and playwright, was Mann's close friend and neighbor in Munich and in California.

5. Heinrich Mann was in France. Peter Pringsheim had dropped out of sight somewhere in Belgium. Nothing had been heard from Golo since he made his way into France at the beginning of the invasion and volunteered as a Red Cross driver. Heinrich and Golo Mann were smuggled across the Pyrenees into Spain and arrived in New York in October.

Kahler to Mann

Woodstock, N.Y.
July 20, 1940[1]

My dear Friend:

Your news was already eagerly awaited, and your letter, troubled through it sounds, was still comforting and warming in its confirmation of our closeness. I need not tell you how hard it has been for *me* to be separated from you for so long at this particular time. What remains to us in this ghastly world except the few people we are attached to? Together with them it is somewhat easier to bear what has to be borne! It moves me to hear you speaking in a way I have not been accustomed to hear from you. For as you know, I've always let you carry me along into more sanguine views; I've always been so grateful for your faith, and often enough I've blamed myself for my skepticism, which I was unable to silence. Deep down I have *never,* since Munich, in fact since Spain, since Baldwin and Blum and more than ever since the first days of Chamberlain and Daladier,[2] believed in a victory of the Allies. The way things have turned out seems to me nothing

[33]

but consistent. I have felt too keenly the way the wind was blowing, have been too conscious of the magnitude of the transformation we are involved in. If I look back now, everything I have undertaken seems to me nothing but an attempt to save, to preserve, to transport what was dear to us, to try to impose some intellectual control on this transformation so that it achieves the goal it will have to reach anyhow. It was a childish endeavor, for upheavals of such dimensions necessarily take the elemental course, setting in motion avalanches of earth and crap. Forgive me for talking this way, although I am well aware that you too have striven toward the same end, both within and outside your writing. Of course it is of no use; we have to face up to that. Yet in spite of everything and no matter what is taking place, I still do believe that it will not have been in vain, some day, beyond our personal selves. Only we cannot spare mankind anything. There was not enough time for preparation and education; there was not enough human room for the urge toward goodness to unfold. The pressure of circumstances and of instincts has been faster and mightier.

Strangely — I myself wonder at this — I am not quite so pessimistic about this country as you are, although I too recognize the danger as enormous. But here I still feel fresh forces of resistance, and their primitive, slumberous quality might as easily serve good as evil. In any case there is some sense to our devoting our ultimate efforts to publicizing the issues here, to awakening people and making them aware of what is at stake; and after all we have nothing else left to do. We ought not and may not give up as long as some short span of life is left to us. But that is also why I think Erika should not go to England. I know her eagerness to throw herself into the fray, and I understand her delight in the venturesome life. But it is already too late for what *she* can do there — or, if we want to be very hopeful, too soon. All we ought to be sending over now are war materials and fliers. I even think they have enough people, but as you know, people are not what count. It is a question of coastal fortifications, of planes and antiaircraft guns. If this equipment functions, the Nazis can never land as many troops as the British have; but if it doesn't function, more men will not help either.

This year we have a much handsomer and very spacious house with a magnificent view over woods and meadows down into the Hudson plain. Unfortunately, it has been mostly cold up to now, and for whole weeks at a time there were torrential thunderstorms and frantic downpours. Now hot weather has arrived at last, and we welcome it. Fine has her ups and downs, but on the whole is not too well. My mother paints peacefully, and there are many guests from New York. I fight my depression with riding and tennis and walks in the woods; as yet I have not accomplished much in the way of work. I wish I had the faculty to make a diversion out of the dreadful state of the world, but my kind of work repeatedly plunges me into the midst of the problems.

I have the sharpest, happiest recollection of the hermit.[3] I would be delighted to enjoy the aftertaste in reading. When will that be possible? Have you gone much further? Ah, if only I could hear how it goes on. It has all along been so comforting in all its bloodiness!

I am very worried about Golo, often dream of him. And I cannot help thinking of your brother also, and of the many friends of whom we have no news. I received a cry for help from a Prague cousin[4] of mine (also a friend of Golo's), from Lisbon. He reached there after a fantastic escape, losing half his family on the way ... All the letters I receive from Switzerland sound like goodbyes. Incidentally, a Milan friend[5] wrote me from there: "In Milan we did not sleep seven nights in a row; Saturday night was the worst ..." There seem to have been very heavy British air raids on the city, but not a word about them in the newspapers.

Please write again soon! All good thoughts and wishes for you and your whole family.

Ever yours,
E. K.

1. *Briefwechsel.*

2. Stanley Baldwin's (1867-1947) third term as British prime minister, 1935-1937, coincided with a deterioration of international relations, the decline of the League of Nations, the rise of Nazi Germany, the Italian conquest of Ethiopia, and the start of the war in Spain. Léon Blum (1872-1950), a Socialist, headed the first Popular Front government in France, 1936-1937, was vice premier 1937-1938, premier briefly in 1938, and opposed the Munich Pact. Arrested in 1940 by the Vichy government, he was imprisoned in Austria until the end of the war. Edouard Daladier (1884-1970) resigned as premier of France in 1934 because of inability to cope with fascist-monarchist riots. Again premier (1938-1940), he signed the Munich Pact and the declaration of war against Germany. He was imprisoned by the Germans until 1945.

3. The reference is to the hermit Kamadamana in Thomas Mann's novella *Die vertauschten Köpfe: Eine Indische Legende* (Stockholm, 1940) (*The Transposed Heads: A Legend of India* [New York, 1941]). On June 12, 1940, Mann "read [his] family and a few friends a new chapter from *The Transposed Heads* (a chapter involving an ascetic in the Indian jungle)" (*Letters,* p. 338).

4. Felix von Kahler, industrialist, brother of the painter Eugen von Kahler, who was a friend of Vasily Kandinsky.

5. Elsa Brinkmann, a Milan physician.

Kahler to Mann

Woodstock, N.Y.
August 29, 1940[1]

My dear Thomas Mann:

Unfortunately I haven't heard from you again — I hope

you received my letter — so don't know whether you are still in California, or already on the way home, or at the Borgi[2] meeting, or somewhere else. I am sending this exploratory note out at random, with a plea for a brief report on how you are and what you have heard about Europe, about Golo, your brother, your brother-in-law. I was in New York recently to meet relatives[3] who had come from France on a small Portuguese ship (although up to now they have got no farther than Ellis Island), and at one point I heard that Erika had flown off, but nothing more . . .

We had a bad summer. I'm not in the mood to tell about it, for who has the right to complain nowadays . . . At any rate, the situation in Europe seems somewhat less dreadful than it did in the spring — at least insofar as we may hope, touch wood, that the victory march is slowed down. Of course that doesn't mean anything but stagnation, disintegration, and a protracted, indescribable misery. But the nations will have to pass through all that.

To my delighted surprise, a new issue of *Mass und Wert*[4] came along recently. Bringing it out should be called a definite victory, for this magazine of ours is more and more becoming a symbol. As long as it waves, there is still one fort on the European continent where our cause is upheld.

Once again I must put before you two selected petitions — I let them speak for themselves, without any extra urging of mine. Still and all, both are worthy of consideration. An Austrian committee has already done something about Gerti Hofmannsthal[5] — but the outcome is highly uncertain.

I have been unable to make up my mind to move to New York and give up the house in Princeton. So we will move in there again around September 20th — I am very impatient to be back with you again, at last.

Until then fond greetings to all of you,

Ever yours,
E. K.

[37]

1. *Briefwechsel.*
2. The Borgeses.
3. Felix von Kahler and his family.
4. Probably the March–April 1940 issue of *Mass und Wert,* Vol. 3, No. 3.
5. Gertrude von Hofmannsthal, née Schlesinger, Hugo von Hofmannsthal's widow. She died in London in 1959. Hugo von Hofmannsthal (1874-1929) was the Austrian poet and playwright who wrote *Elektra* (1903), *Ödipus und die Sphinx* (1905), *Ariadne auf Naxos* (1912), and the libretto for Richard Strauss's *Der Rosenkavalier.*

Mann to Kahler

Los Angeles
September 5, 1940[1]

Dear friend Kahler:

No, it isn't nice that you have heard nothing from us all this time, ever since our letters at the beginning of the summer. But these months were so preoccupied, so filled with affairs — and mostly the kind of sad affairs that accord with these times. There was the struggle to rescue Golo and my brother from France, a struggle that hasn't *yet* been effectual; there were the constant efforts for all the others in danger over there — we have been living with cries for help ringing in our ears from all the unfortunates (who had wanted to go on being Europeans for too long — sheer self-indulgence), and for a long time our house literally resembled an Emergency Rescue Office. Then there was a great deal of socializing, then the effort to keep my personal work going, which was successful to a degree. For after completing the Indian jest, I once more took in hand the threads of the *Joseph,* which had been left lying for so long, and a few chapters of the new volume [*Joseph the Provider*] can stand. In short, little energy was left for correspondence, that is, for letters to dear friends.

We parted heavy-heartedly with Erika; it was a harrowing experience. But then again I am proud of the brave child and cannot be angry with her. She is also *clever* and *lucky,* and I trust that we will have a happy reunion in November.

According to the official view here, exiles in England are not in *imminent danger.* For that reason it is difficult to bring people over from there, and the case of Gerti Hofmannsthal will also present complications. But an attempt should certainly be made.

The thing Donath[2] is advocating impresses me favorably, and leaving aside all the caution I have learned, I see no reason for not signing as a *sponsor* if Beer-Hofmann[3] is doing the same. Couldn't we postpone the decision until our return? If that isn't feasible, I am ready under the above mentioned condition.

Our stay here — the entire summer was wonderfully brisk and sunny — is approaching its end. On October 4 we will leave, will again spend a day in Chicago, and from there go straight back to Stockhaldi[4] (as I say this I recall that the Schiedhaldi[5] was recently rented out; it gave me a twinge). We could have heard no better news than that you too will again be taking your house there. So we shall celebrate Christmas together, and *if* England (for which my admiration grows daily) is still standing then, it will not be a hopeless Christmas. You are probably right: all we can hope for at the present time is for the triumphant advance of the evil one to come to a halt. But so long as the monster's victory is not complete, isn't that enough for it slowly but surely to become defeat? It seems as if this country has only wanted to make sure of the British will to resist. I think that whether Willkie or F.D.R. wins,[6] if England survives the winter we'll have America in the war in the spring. And then the invasion of Europe will scarcely be necessary. What the beast carefully avoided mentioning in his last "speech" is the obvious consolidation of the English-speaking world. Which the Germans are interpreting as a sellout of the Empire in exchange for old ships — a whimsical misjudgment of the situation, without a doubt.

I too was delighted with the new issue of M.u.W. [*Mass und Wert*] and was literally shaken by the Gentz preface of 1805,[7] which was Golo's last cannon shot and which you must read! One finds oneself continually underlining phrases that seem coined for present circumstances. And what a German they wrote in those days!

Keep well! Let us look forward to our reunion!

Yours,

Thomas Mann

The 6th

A letter from Oprecht prompts me to reopen this letter. He asks for material for the last issue of the year — which he still wants to publish — probably as the last one altogether. He has a contribution from me and one from Ernst Bloch, also a number of things he has rounded up himself.[8] Couldn't you send him something from your papers, lectures, drafts — a few pages or even more than a few? You were in it at the beginning —don't you want to be in at the presumptive end also? I would be grateful.

The postponement of the discussion of universal military service in Congress on the motion of a labeled Nazi like H. Fish[9] is a frightful symptom of the country's condition. Unfortunately, there can be no doubt that in acting this way Congress has the great masses of the population behind it, despite the clear insight of the intellectuals. So much the worse when one finds that all the optimism one has sincerely mustered, the kind of optimism expressed in my remarks yesterday, is repeatedly put to shame and struck down. Rumania, too, is cheerful.[10] And I certainly don't overlook the fact that England is pretty hopelessly on the defensive. Very well, then, the advance has *not* been stopped. We are probably misreading our lot when we imagine that we shall ever again be allowed to draw a joyful breath. And yet we are, after all, better, finer, superior human beings— or aren't we? What does it signify when everything is against us and all satisfaction is denied us? Surely one has the right to ask.

1. *Briefwechsel.*

2. Ludwig Donath (b. 1906), Austrian actor, emigrated to the United States in 1939 and appeared in American films and television and on the Broadway stage.

3. Richard Beer-Hofmann (1886-1945), Austrian poet, playwright, and novelist, a member of the Young Vienna group of writers, emigrated in 1938 to Switzerland, then to the United States.

4. The Manns' rented house on Stockton Street in Princeton. It now bears a large plaque (the gift of Caroline Newton [b. 1893], psychoanalyst and translator, who was a friend of the Manns), stating that Thomas Mann lived there.

5. The Manns' rented house on Schiedhaldenstrasse in the Zurich suburb of Küsnacht.

6. Wendell Lewis Willkie (1892-1944), lawyer and corporation president, the Republican nominee for President of the United States in 1940, was defeated by Franklin Delano Roosevelt.

7. Friedrich Gentz, "Vorrede der 'Fragmente zur Geschichte des europäischen Gleichgewichts,'" *Mass und Wert,* 3 (May–June–July 1940). Friedrich von Gentz (1764-1832), friend and adviser of Metternich, was the chief secretary of important European congresses.

8. Ernst Bloch (b. 1885), university professor and philosophical writer, emigrated to the United States in 1939 and returned to Germany in 1949. See Mann to Kahler, September 25, 1940, note 3.

9. Hamilton Fish (b. 1888), congressman from New York, 1920-1945, was a leading isolationalist and anti-Communist who was once accused of having connections with the Bundists and other Axis supporters.

10. In the summer of 1940, parts of Rumania were annexed by Russia, Bulgaria, and Hungary.

Mann to Kahler

Brentwood
September 25, 1940[1]

Dear Kahler:

First of all some joyful news: A few days ago we at last had the longed-for telegram from Lisbon. Heinrich and Golo have both arrived there safely. It is only a smaller step from there to us, and they may even reach New York before we do. I cannot leave here before October 6 because of a lecture commitment. But Klaus, at least, will be on the spot.

I am enclosing a few lines on Canetti's[2] behalf. I remember we talked about him earlier, and have always been ready to provide an affidavit for the author of *Die Blendung,* which at the time made a remarkable impression upon me. It isn't quite clear to me whether Canetti is still in Vienna or in England. I thought at the time we talked about him that he was still in Austria, but I believe I've since heard that he reached England. In the brief affidavit I have therefore deliberately expressed myself vaguely on this point.

Although I am sorry I cannot join the Donath effort to the extent of appearing together with our Beer-Hofmann, I shouldn't want to withhold my "protectorate," since the thing is clearly innocuous. Please tell Donath, therefore, that I gladly place my name at his disposal, but that I shall be able to devote scarcely any time to the cause.

Oprecht wrote me today about the next issue of *Mass und Wert.* He has all sorts of material for it. Aside from the beginning of my Indian novella, he is also publishing — with the permission of the Swiss censorship — Raymond Gram Swing's speech, something by Ernst Bloch, an essay by Schirokauer on semantic transformation of the novel. Professor Karl Löwenstein has promised something on political symbolism, and Silone a selection from his new novel.[3] There are also several critical articles at hand. I need not repeat how desirable it would be if you were to contribute something. I think if you could send it off immediately after your return to Princeton (which I suppose will be in the next few days), it would not be too late.

Looking forward to seeing you soon! Cordially,

T. M

The letter was left unmailed, and meanwhile yours arrived. There is something to it — that we are thinking of a later move to California — although it has not yet been definitely decided. But in any case we shall be spending the winter in Princeton. We've had very bad news: the unfortunate Lanyis[4] were on the torpedoed ship bound for Canada. Moni was saved and brought back to England, but her husband drowned. Their marriage was extraordinarily happy, and it is hardly conceivable that the poor child can recover from this shock and the terrible strains that those who were saved were exposed to for many hours. She was taken first to a hospital in Scotland, and Erika, who cabled us about the disaster, was just about to fetch her from there — which at any rate means Moni is able to travel. We are now waiting for further news.

1. *Briefwechsel.*

2. Elias Canetti (b. 1905), writer, fled from Vienna to England. His novel *Die Blendung* was first published in 1935.

3. *Mass und Wert,* 3 (September–October–November 1940), contained Ignazio Silone's "Esel, Bauern und Redner," Arno Schirokauer's "Bedeutungswandel des Romans," Raymond Gram Swing's "Jugend, Krieg und Freiheit," and Ernst Bloch's "Über das noch nicht bewusste Wissen." The beginning of *The Transposed Heads* was not published, nor was Karl Löwenstein's work on political symbolism. Raymond Gram Swing (1887-1968), the noted American journalist, radio news commentator, and author, during the war commented on American affairs for the British Broadcasting Corporation, and on foreign affairs

for the Mutual Broadcasting System and the American Broadcasting Company. Karl Löwenstein (in America, Loewenstein; 1891-1973) at one time served as legal adviser to the Manns in Germany; he was professor of political science at Amherst College, 1936-1961, and the author of numerous books, including *Political Power and the Governmental Process* (Chicago, 1957).

4. Mann's daughter Monika (b. 1910) was married to Jenö Lanyi (1902-1940), a Hungarian art historian. He drowned during the sinking of the British evacuation ship *City of Benares*. Monika (Moni) Lanyi wrote *Past and Present* (1960), a memoir of her childhood and later life.

Mann to Kahler

Hotel Durant
Berkeley, California
March 30, 1941[1]

Dear friend Kahler:

Let me send you melancholic and cordial greetings from the midst of a persisting wretched turmoil. Many adventures already lie between our parting and today, all stalwartly and bravely fought through. Chicago with Medi, Borgi, and the baby was peaceable and familial. Erika joined us there. The anti-Papist[2] read powerfully from his Mexican opera libretto[3] (in English), and I produced the dream-interpretation chapter,[4] which made the children laugh until they cried. Then came Colorado Springs and Denver — at the altitude of St. Moritz and therefore somewhat taxing. Colorado Springs must be a charming place in weather other than the kind we had almost all the time: rain and rain. Here too. The journey from Denver to Los Angeles took 36 hours. We found the Franks in the hotel; then my brother arrived — I having to change in the midst of all this to deliver my lecture. We stayed up late; we had to be up at five o'clock the next morning to catch the plane for San Francisco. The two-hour flight, with an excellent breakfast above the clouds and the magnificent mountains, was a remarkable experience. Another was being fetched from the airport by a police guard and being driven with sirens howling through all the lights. A new experience for me. Here, we are having fine, uproarious celebrations — too many of them. The ceremony on the campus, scenically perhaps the loveliest in the world, was for once favored by the weather; the sun shone and the big amphitheater, seen from the stage (where we again met Katia's brother), made a delightful, colorful picture. And so I have now become a doctor of laws, again something new; but I don't notice the difference. The Freemason-like induction into the chapter of Phi Beta Kappa (Philosophia Biou Kybernetes) was majestic; thereafter came a grand banquet, and then when sensible folk would have gone to bed, my lecture took place, in two overcrowded halls, one where I spoke and another that was served by a loudspeaker. I had made appropriate changes in the text and talked about the thinker's responsibility for life, which had been lacking in Germany, and also about Nietzsche, saying that were he alive he would be in America today and American tolerance would likewise have inducted him into the Phi Beta Kappa fraternity, in spite of his romantic sins.[5] That brought laughter.

We are staying here a few days longer than planned. It is more sensible to go to Stanford University first and from there to Carmel. We shall be returning to Los Angeles about the 8th or the 9th and will then take refuge in the cottage at 740 Amalfi Drive, Brentwood.

The beast is not doing anything against the Serbs. He "will not let himself be provoked"[6] — too bad. The American confiscation of the ships[7] is certainly a cheering stroke — still barely *short of war*. But the British shipping losses must be dreadful, and although things go well in the Mediterranean and the "Axis" is by now no more than a name for the "maintenance of order" in Italy, we must arm ourselves against terrible blows still to come.

Cordially yours,
Thomas Mann

1. *Letters.*

2. Mann's son-in-law, G. A. Borgese.

3. *Montezuma,* a dramatic poem set to music by Roger Sessions; the premiere was given by the Berlin State Opera in the spring of 1964.

4. In *Joseph the Provider.*

5. "Denken und Leben," presented in German, March 27, 1941 ("Thinking and Living," in *Order of the Day*).

6. The reference is to the military coup in Belgrade and the popular uprising throughout the country on March 27, 1941. The regent Paul, who had been subservient to the Germans, was deposed, and King Peter II was declared no longer a minor and given power to form a new government. On April 6, Hitler nevertheless allowed himself to be "provoked" and began his war against Yugoslavia.

7. The Axis powers, Germany and Italy, had repeatedly violated American neutrality at sea. As a reprisal, and on suspicion of sabotage, German and Italian merchant vessels were detained in the ports of the United States.

Kahler to Mann

May 23, 1941[1]

My dear Friend:

It is disgraceful that I am only now sitting down to answer your good and prompt report. And it is totally absurd that I have not written for so long, since I have been *continually* thinking of you and Katia with longing and a keen sense of deprivation during this once again frightful spring. Hundreds of times I have had the impulse to lift the receiver and call 1068 — a dear and familiar reaction to all events — and a sinister silence lurks in the telephone corner since I can no longer do that.

Still and all, I could not bring myself to write, perhaps for that very reason. For everything has been so dreary and depressing these past months, and the sort of thing one tends to say in such moods evaporates as soon as we are in contact with each other and is not exactly what one likes to write down and set out in black and white. And so one lets it pass and waits for an upbeat of some kind. I had to summon up all my strength to go through with my weekly "juggling act" at the New School [for Social Research]: forty English pages of storming through world history. I have to write them in four days and sometimes nights, and then memorize the whole thing so that it will seem easily tossed off in a chatty fashion. That is quite a job for such an unchatty fellow as I am — I really could not help being amazed at myself. But finally it turned out very well; my twenty-five students, among them a Chinese and a Hindu, stuck with me right to the end and seemed quite pleased with the presentation. Next year I have to give a course through both semesters, thirty lectures; I am slightly aghast at the prospect. In Detroit, too, I performed once and am also to have a short cycle there next year. There I even climbed to the heights of receiving $50 per lecture. All this might be worth thinking about — and incidentally I have even managed in this way to draft an outline of my long planned history of man,[2] which I now want to present to a publisher and the Guggenheim [Foundation]; it would all be acceptable if the times were different. But as things are, all this cannot stem the profound melancholy that creeps over me at the realization that we apparently can do very little about stopping the "wave of the future."[3] And although we know that it *cannot* be the future of mankind, it may be ours unless something fundamental changes very rapidly right here, and unfortunately I see no signs of that. Things are very bad in this country, and that is the bitterest part of it. *A qui le dis-je*. So enough of that.

I have not seen much of people because of strenuous work, and unfortunately much too little of Golo also since he has been in New York. He was here once and is to come out to see me again next week. The summer is still uncertain. My mother could probably go to Woodstock again with Beer-Hofmann. I myself want to take a small trip with Fine — she has again had a very bad spell, poor thing. Unfortunately, in view of my obligations for next winter it's highly questionable whether there will be any time left for California. I am going to have to do a great deal of preparatory work.

Please write soon and do not retaliate for my silence! How is the house going? Is it building? And how far has the *Joseph* come? What a pity that I am no longer permitted to keep up with it. Fond, fond greetings to you and Katia, to whom I also mean to write shortly. Perhaps one of these days she will favor me with one of her scoldings — I miss them so much.

Ever yours,

E. K.

1. *Briefwechsel*.
2. *Man the Measure*.
3. An allusion to Anne Morrow Lindbergh's *The Wave of the Future* (1940), which advocated strict isolationism for the United States.

Mann to Kahler

Pacific Palisades, California
May 25, 1941[1]

Dear friend Kahler:

What is going on? Why haven't we heard anything from you for such a long time, literally since we parted? Something is wrong, and if you replied, "Why, I haven't heard from you," it would come to light that the letter I sent you en route, during our journey, has been lost, and that you had thought all along, "Out of sight, out of mind." It would be sad if you could possibly have taken this notion into your head. I no longer remember from what stage of the trip I wrote you. Perhaps from Colorado Springs, where I had a desk? But I did write — pages and pages — and we have often asked ourselves since: Why hasn't he written even once? For we often speak of you among ourselves, since we have the habit of comparing everyone here with whom we are on a friendly footing with you and saying, "But Kahler was better!" or "Everything would be fine if only Kahler were here!" Believe it or not.

Of course there may have been other reasons for your silence, e.g., the formidable burden of work with your lectures. The series[2] was concluded on a highly successful note, I hear. I have great respect for what you have accomplished, especially since you found you had to speak extemporaneously. You have given an example of fortitude that honorably differs from the complete incompetence of most refugee intellectuals faced with their new situation. None of them, I have the impression, is prepared to learn anything new; rather they all want to go on as they did in times now buried, and expect roasted squabs to fly into their mouths. Didn't Golo write that you have been invited to lecture in the Middle West? And what has been arranged with the New School for the next academic year?

Are you very depressed by events, i.e., by our constant defeats? That, too, would be sufficient reason for your silence. I often wonder at the phlegmatic disposition, a peculiar mixture of contempt and confidence, with which I take all this without especially allowing it to disturb my work. Perhaps the sunniness and vividness of this region, this easy living and somewhat slack oversized seaside resort, are helpful. Also we are inured — or numbed — to "taking" it, and a kind of permanent muscular contraction has developed, so that we receive but don't really feel the successive blows. Enough; I live from day to day, and meantime pile one page of *Joseph* upon the other. I am in the middle of the grand dialogue — a whole series of chapters — between Joseph and Pharaoh Amenhotep, which will lead by roundabout and hermetically cunning ways to Joseph's elevation. You'd like it, I think. I recently read to Erika and my wife for hours, and once again "dear Erich" was very much missed.

As in the East, there is no lack of interruptions and episodes here. There have been the celebration of my brother's seventieth birthday, the monthly messages to Germany, which I now put on records at the N.B.C. studio for London, a grand dinner and speech for the Federal Union in the Beverly Hills Hotel, and early in June I have to go to San Francisco for a meeting organized by the Emergency Rescue Committee, to which Kingdon[3] will be coming also. My speech is ready and recounts quite bluntly what stupidity, baseness, and ignorance we exiles have had to endure from the world for eight long years.[4] I must say, I am looking forward to getting this off my chest.

Here we are living in a pretty, very sensible, and practical little house in a rural setting, and we shall spend at least the summer in it. Our plans for building have been subject to many vacillations — not only the plans, but even the very intention to build. That is to say, *we* were the ones who ander; it blooms very beautifully. Only I have a suspicion that it may do so all year round.

Day before yesterday we visited Claremont — Pomona College — to ingratiate ourselves there for Golo's sake. When he comes west he must also call there and put on his most polished manners. His French credentials made an impression after all. We heard and read the FDR speech with feelings similar to yours. This emphasis on the "Hemisphere" instead of on England and the English-speaking world was distasteful to me. Halifax[2] was not invited, but the ambassadors of those filthy fascistic South American republics were, and Argentina has promptly disavowed the "Hemisphere" and declared her neutrality. Moreover, deeds are singularly lacking, and even under the *unlimited emergency* Lindbergh has been allowed to talk again,[3] which I would not have thought possible. Twenty-five million dollars' worth of *supplies for Britain* goes up in flames, and they say there must be no jumping to conclusions. No, things are in a bad way — unfortunately you are right about that. For the present England can expect only further defeats, and if America cannot be roused, we may well come to the point of asking ourselves whether we are not going to lose this campaign.

Yours,
Thomas Mann

1. *Letters.*
2. Edward Frederick, Earl of Halifax (1881–1959), was British ambassador in Washington, 1941–1946.
3. Charles Augustus Lindbergh (b. 1902), who in 1927 had made the first solo nonstop transatlantic flight, from New York to Paris, was making isolationist and antiwar speeches.

vacillated, which is understandable in these times, and given the uncertainty of the future. At one point we had definitely decided *not* to build, to pay off the architect and withdraw. But now it seems after all as if we will begin and from the autumn on live under our own — that is, under the Federal Loan's — roof. The thing appears more risky than it is. Rents will rise. Actually, we will live more cheaply than in the kind of rented house we would need in the long run, and the site is so beautiful that we can rent or sell at any time. The East is not lost to us. A lecture tour there for late fall is already being arranged. So we shall see you again!

Erika is with us and has been a real comfort — enlivening, entertaining, helpful — a dear, strong child. Only she is very anxious, as we are too, about Klaus, who is having ominous, exhausting problems with his magazine.[5] We have done everything possible to raise money to help him — with minimal success.

How is your poor dear Fine? My wife is very concerned about her too and would like to have her address.

Yours,
Thomas Mann

1. *Letters.*
2. Lectures at the New School for Social Research in 1940–1941, which later became the basis of Kahler's book *Man the Measure.*
3. Frank Kingdon (1894-1972), university professor, radio commentator, and writer, was the chairman of the International Rescue Committee and other organizations and worked with Thomas Mann on a plan to issue twenty-four pamphlets written by members of the German intelligentsia for the Germans.
4. "Vor dem American Rescue Committee," in *Altes und Neues: Kleine Prosa aus fünf Jahrzehnten* (Frankfurt, 1953).
5. *Decision: A Review of Free Culture.* The magazine, founded and edited by Klaus Mann, lasted from January 1941 to February 1942.

vacillated, which is understandable in these times, and given the uncertainty of the future. At one point we had definitely decided *not* to build, to pay off the architect and withdraw. But now it seems after all as if we will begin and from the autumn on live under our own — that is, under the Federal Loan's — roof. The thing appears more risky than it is. Rents will rise. Actually, we will live more cheaply than in the kind of rented house we would need in the long run, and the site is so beautiful that we can rent or sell at any time. The East is not lost to us. A lecture tour there for late fall is already being arranged. So we shall see you again!

Erika is with us and has been a real comfort — enlivening, entertaining, helpful — a dear, strong child. Only she is very anxious, as we are too, about Klaus, who is having ominous, exhausting problems with his magazine.[5] We have done everything possible to raise money to help him — with minimal success.

How is your poor dear Fine? My wife is very concerned about her too and would like to have her address.

Yours,
Thomas Mann

1. *Letters.*

2. Lectures at the New School for Social Research in 1940–1941, which later became the basis of Kahler's book *Man the Measure.*

3. Frank Kingdon (1894-1972), university professor, radio commentator, and writer, was the chairman of the International Rescue Committee and other organizations and worked with Thomas Mann on a plan to issue twenty-four pamphlets written by members of the German intelligentsia for the Germans.

4. "Vor dem American Rescue Committee," in *Altes und Neues: Kleine Prosa aus fünf Jahrzehnten* (Frankfurt, 1953).

5. *Decision: A Review of Free Culture.* The magazine, founded and edited by Klaus Mann, lasted from January 1941 to February 1942.

Kahler to Mann

310 Nassau Street
Princeton, New Jersey
May 28, 1941[1]

Dear Thomas Mann:

Your dear and moving letter has just arrived, crossed with mine, which I mailed at the end of last week. I hope it has reached you. To my distress I have realized that Amalfi Drive is located in Pacific Palisades and not in Los Angeles — Brentwood, where I addressed it. But I trust that the letter reached you anyway, since I imagine the coast out there is like the Côte d'Azur or Lake Como, where the names also change every few kilometers and yet it's the same. But please do write me a line to confirm whether you have received the letter, since I don't want to repeat my account. If the letter hasn't reached you, I'll write again *by return mail* and at length. I am doubly ashamed of my long epistolary paralysis — that is going to change!

Golo has just come for a few days, and yesterday we listened to the President together.[2] Neither of us had a good impression of the speech; it corroborates in content, in style, and in the delivery a lack of elasticity which is doubly and triply necessary now, when the war is really only just starting. It is what I already feared at the time of the election: he is somewhat exhausted. A man with a conscience and constitutional restrictions, which means one with constant internal and external frictions, simply cannot come through eight such years like a manic criminal who goes speeding over hill and dale and therefore really, in a sense — in more than one sense — acts like a "sleepwalker." Oh well, since he's already cracked, let's hope he cracks up!

Do you by any chance have a copy of the speech in San Francisco which you could send me, even if only on loan? I am very eager to read it.

[52]

All the rest was in my letter. Fine's address is Hotel Walton, 104 West 70th Street, N.Y.C.

Warmest regards to Katia and Erika.

Ever yours,

E. K.

1. Thomas Mann Archives, Zurich.

2. On May 27, 1941, Roosevelt proclaimed an unlimited national emergency. The statutes dealing with such an emergency served to concentrate vast powers in the President.

Mann to Kahler

740 Amalfi Drive
Pacific Palisades
June 1, 1941[1]

Dear Kahler:

All is well; the first as well as the second letter has arrived and I am once more up to date. My wife, now that she has the address, will write to Fine shortly.

Your notion of the townships here and their names is exactly right. We ourselves were of the belief, at first, that we belonged to Brentwood, and added Los Angeles to our address for good measure, but were repeatedly corrected by the post office until we resigned ourselves to living nowhere else but in Pacific Palisades, California, although I did not consider that a town name at all, and in fact it probably isn't a township but a landscape with a few colonial homes and an ocean view.

In this, my favorite season of the year, it is also lovely here, although I liked it better in Küsnacht and even in Princeton. Here everything blooms in violet and grape colors that look rather made of paper, and because they're a bit too fancy I don't quite fancy them. But I do fancy the oleander; it blooms very beautifully. Only I have a suspicion that it may do so all year round.

Day before yesterday we visited Claremont — Pomona College — to ingratiate ourselves there for Golo's sake. When he comes west he must also call there and put on his most polished manners. His French credentials made an impression after all. We heard and read the FDR speech with feelings similar to yours. This emphasis on the "Hemisphere" instead of on England and the English-speaking world was distasteful to me. Halifax[2] was not invited, but the ambassadors of those filthy fascistic South American republics were, and Argentina has promptly disavowed the "Hemisphere" and declared her neutrality. Moreover, deeds are singularly lacking, and even under the *unlimited emergency* Lindbergh has been allowed to talk again,[3] which I would not have thought possible. Twenty-five million dollars' worth of *supplies for Britain* goes up in flames, and they say there must be no jumping to conclusions. No, things are in a bad way — unfortunately you are right about that. For the present England can expect only further defeats, and if America cannot be roused, we may well come to the point of asking ourselves whether we are not going to lose this campaign.

Yours,
Thomas Mann

1. *Letters.*

2. Edward Frederick, Earl of Halifax (1881–1959), was British ambassador in Washington, 1941–1946.

3. Charles Augustus Lindbergh (b. 1902), who in 1927 had made the first solo nonstop transatlantic flight, from New York to Paris, was making isolationist and antiwar speeches.

Mann to Kahler

Pacific Palisades
December 31, 1941[1]

Dear friend Kahler:

For the New Year I want to wish you and Fine and your dear mother good fortune and health; not to do so would be a cold, unpleasant thing, and I am sure you too are wishing us the best tonight, even if you don't manage to set it down on paper. We are both *desperately busy* and therefore bad correspondents. For Christmas we made it a bit easier for ourselves by sending greetings by telegram. We told you, most sincerely, that we missed you, and have heard much the same from you. Where did you spend Christmas Eve — in New York or Princeton? It is truly a constant source of surprise, the places where we spend our days. On the twenty-fourth I went walking without an overcoat on my favorite promenade above the ocean, sat a long while on a bench in the sun — it is bearable at this season — and looked dreamily out at the blue theater of war.

I have been presented with an electric clock which I admire every morning, wondering how it contrives overnight to straighten out its calendar. How does the beast know that from the 29th to the 30th it has to change both figures, but from the 30th to the 31st only the second, and that from the 31st to the 1st the first has to vanish? It comprehends what is necessary, and I cannot understand how. But at the end of February we will certainly have to come to its aid.

Let me not forget your cake, which I think is the richest I have ever encountered in this category. It can scarcely still be called a cake, and confirms the saying that everything supreme of its kind goes beyond its kind.

Nothing came of our hopes to spend Christmas in Seven Palms House.[2] But it is almost done; we shall be able to move in by the second half of January, and I shall, Heil Hitler, have the finest study I have ever worked in. Everything, in fact merely the floor coverings, runs into unnerving sums of money, and if I had not recently become Consultant in Germanic Literature[3] to the Library of Congress, with a small annual salary, I wouldn't know how we were going to manage. Had you heard about that yet? But I have the appointment and will occasionally have to deliver a lecture there.

We must only hope that the strip of coast will not be evacuated some day, with Seven Palms House becoming the quarters of some American colonel or perhaps later the Mikado! Americans are having bitter experiences. They never really believed in ours; at bottom they thought we were telling atrocity stories. How could we help laughing bitterly when Hull said of the last Japanese note that such lying and deceit had never happened before?[4] It happened twenty-five times before, but no one wanted to or could recognize it. My Diotima, Mrs. Meyer,[5] told me she hoped I was not suffering too much from all this. I answered her: "Dear Madam, I suffered *before,* when it was still tactless to show your suffering. Now I feel rather good." Of course it's impossible to feel very good about the outcome of such incredible carelessness. But there is almost nothing that in the proper circumstances cannot be set right. For the coming year we can rationally only wish and hope that things will not go so badly that they cannot sometime go better and finally go well again.

Have you read former Ambassador Davies' *Mission to Moscow?*[6] An excellent book, essentially made up of his reports to Washington and extracts from a diary. But what clarity and foresight! No other diplomat has sent such reports home about Russia. America, it seems, has long been the only country the Russians trusted. Incidentally, in 1939, Roosevelt sent word to Stalin that if he really concluded a pact with Hitler, as certainly as day follows night H. would attack Russia after crushing France.

Over the holidays our little house was stuffed full. In addition to Golo, Erika was here, animating as ever, and my brother-in-law from Berkeley.[7] Then our little grandson, whom we took along with us from San Francisco for a few weeks to relieve his mother — a charming child, highly nervous, so it seems to me, but as such things go, on this very account particularly witty and winning.[8]

Yesterday I made my German phonograph record[9] again, and was particularly insulting toward Schicklgruber.[10] It does the heart good.

I am making steady progress on *Joseph*. At bottom the dialogue with Pharaoh has not turned out as I had promised myself. I am therefore taking all the more pains with the following section. It is the story of Tamar, a big insert, practically a novella in itself. Do you recall? A remarkable female who shrank from nothing in order to thrust her way into the sacred story. I cannot read enough of *Faust* and everything else that has been done along those lines, for after all I have a kind of universal poem under my hands, although only a humorous and bizarre one. I have never thought myself great, but I love to play with greatness and to live on a certain footing of familiarity with it.

Yours,

T. M.

1. *Letters.*

2. The house at 1550 San Remo Drive, Pacific Palisades, California, which the Manns were having built.

3. The appointment came on December 1, 1941. From 1941 to 1944, Thomas Mann received $4800 annually. He then waived the honorarium, but continued to hold the post until his death.

4. Cordell Hull (1871-1955) was United States Secretary of State, 1933-1944. One hour after the surprise Japanese attack on American bases in the Pacific, December 7, 1941, a note was delivered by the

Japanese ambassador rejecting the American peace formula of November 26, which included a mutual nonaggression pact. The note accused the United States and Britain of obstructing peace between Japan and China, encircling Japan, and scheming to extend the war.

5. Agnes E. Meyer (1887-1970), the wife of Eugene Meyer, publisher of the *Washington Post,* was a journalist, author of books, and occasional translator of Thomas Mann's articles. During the latter part of his life Thomas Mann corresponded with her more frequently than with anyone else. In Plato's *Symposium,* Socrates refers to a priestess named Diotima as his teacher.

6. Joseph E. Davies (1876-1958) was American ambassador to Moscow, 1936-1938. His book *Mission to Moscow* (1941) lent significant impetus to the American-Russian alliance during the war. In 1943, Davies served as President Roosevelt's special envoy, and in 1945 as envoy for the Potsdam Conference.

7. Peter Pringsheim, the physicist.

8. Fridolin, the son of Michael Mann, Thomas Mann's youngest son, and Gret Moser Mann. Frido was the model for Echo in *Doctor Faustus.* Michael (Bibi) Mann (b. 1919), after a career as a violinist and violist, became a professor of German at Berkeley.

9. Recordings of radio addresses to Germany, subsequently published as *Listen, Germany!* (New York, 1943).

10. Adolf Hitler.

Kahler to Mann

January 27, 1942[1]

My dear Friend:

It is disgraceful — that is gradually getting to be a traditional opening of my letters! But it *is* disgraceful that in this Christmas and New Year season I have not communicated at greater length and more directly with you, and moreover have fallen in debt to you, Katia, and Golo too, for so many precious letters. I am thoroughly ashamed, and it has to be said again each time; each time I have to beat my breast again, although some day I shall have to become resigned to being in permanent arrears, in this department at any rate. It really depresses me, but I don't know what to do about it. The days, weeks, months fly, and my pace, which America has managed to impose on me, always proves too slow to keep up with the demands. A new semester looms before me, with nothing but brand-new *lectures,* and because I have my eye on the book,[2] I cannot refrain from elaborating them far more luxuriantly than is necessary. Incidentally, this unlucrative and informal work is beginning to grow into a kind of regular teaching position, to the extent that I must also read and mark papers. My mother unfortunately began the year with a case of bronchitis; we've laboriously managed to pull her through that. On the other hand, one pleasant but quite difficult matter was a big essay on the fundamental evil of contemporary democracy that I did during the Christmas holidays for the *American Scholar,* and which, if all goes well, will be suitably emasculated and published too late. And so a sluggish man's time passes.

Incidentally, I'd like to turn this essay into a pamphlet or perhaps even a book — rage over our side's continual and incredible mistakes is making it swell from day to day. I can see that I shall be brushing aside all warnings to be careful and will interfere where I have no business to. But sooner or later someone has to say bluntly what the situation of democracy is today, and what straits it will be in if there isn't a thoroughgoing reform. After all, it is a world-wide concern we are all bitterly involved in, with suffering and hopes, and we can legitimately claim the right to define the brand of democracy that we believe in.

People here have connected your name with the committee Mr. Grzesinsky[3] seems to have thought it incumbent upon him to set up. Wrongly so, I very much hope. *Please* do not become involved with these people! Everything possible should be done to discredit these vapid, incompetent petty miscreants.

When I see the arrogance of all these pretenders, including Rauschning, Strasser and Loewenstein,[4] I always have to think of our Jemal Pasha,[5] whom we kept hidden in M[unich] for several months, you know. He was at any rate a person of a different stature and had a better "record" than all these gentlemen, moreover did some exceedingly useful work for his country after his fall. But he always insisted that his public career must be ended, that young, unknown, unencumbered people must be the ones to revive Turkey. And at that time he was only forty-six years old and kicked like a colt out of sheer desire for action.

In spite of everything the world at the beginning of this year is beginning to look somewhat more matutinal again. Now the beast has what he wanted to avoid: the viscous, unpredictable, bogged-down situation of the First World War, if not something worse. He cannot seriously believe that he will defeat Russia, England, and a still wholly fresh America. You are right: simple material superiority will eventually have to do the trick, despite the squandering of energies. Though where would we be without the Russians! (I haven't read Davies yet, but I have read Shirer,[6] who seems to me greatly overestimated.)

You can imagine with what anxiety we have watched the war flare up on your coast, of all places. I hope the effects and restrictions there remain within the previous limits, so that you can enjoy your finest study in tranquillity. I assume you have just moved into it. I am burning with eagerness for more Joseph, but he goes his way far from me. What pleases me most about your new honorary post in Washington, aside from the fact itself, is that it includes a tie to the East. After all, you will have to turn up here fairly often.

Princeton lies covered with snow and quietude, a symbol of the life I am leading here. My social relations have shifted entirely to New York, where I spend a few days every week.

Hardly anyone is left here aside from the insipid Oppenheim, dull Morgenstern, and similar creatures. This year I've scarcely seen the Lowes;[7] they are preoccupied with a grandchild. The only acquisition is the Romance languages man Bonfante,[8] a vital, witty, intellectual Paganini who keeps me entertained. On the whole I like it this way: this beautiful house has become a hermitage for work in which I come to my senses — a rare thing in these times and in this world.

Please don't retaliate for my procrastinating, and write again — your letters are one of the few joys I have.

Letters to Katia and Golo will really follow immediately.

Ever yours,

E. K.

1. Thomas Mann Archives, Zurich.

2. *Man the Measure.*

3. Albert Carl Grzesinsky (b. 1879), writer and politician, who had held numerous offices in Germany, was president of the Advisory Committee for German Refugees.

4. Hermann Rauschning (b. 1887), president of the senate of the Free City of Danzig until 1936, broke with Hitler and fled to Switzerland, then to France, to England, and, in 1941, to the United States. Otto Strasser (b. 1897), a newspaper editor and author of books who had been a member of the Nazi party, broke with Hitler in 1930, was exiled in 1933, and after living in Vienna, Prague, Zurich, and Paris, fled to Canada after the fall of France. Prince Hubertus zu Loewenstein (b. 1906), special adviser to the West German Government Press and Information Office since 1960 and member of parliament from 1953 to 1957, was visiting professor of history and political science, Carnegie Endowment for International Peace, 1937-1946, and founder of the American Guild for German Cultural Freedom.

5. Ahmet Jemal Pasha (1872-1922), a Turkish army officer who was a member of the triumvirate that dominated Turkey during World War I, escaped to Germany when the Ottoman empire was defeated in 1918. He later returned and was murdered. At the request of the government, because he spoke French but not German, in 1919 he was a guest, incognito, at the Kahler villa, St. Georg, in Wolfratshausen, near Munich.

[61]

6. William L. Shirer (b. 1904), American journalist, war corre-
spondent and political commentator for the Columbia Broadcasting
System, wrote *Berlin Diary* (1941) and *The Rise and Fall of the
Third Reich* (1960).

7. Helen T. Lowe-Porter (1877-1963) was the translator of most
of Mann's works. See John C. Thirlwall, *In Another Language: A
Record of the Thirty-Year Relationship between Thomas Mann and
His English Translator, Helen Tracy Lowe-Porter* (New York, 1966).
Her husband, Elias Lowe, the paleographer, taught at Oxford and
Princeton.

8. Giuliano Bonfante (b. 1904, Italy) taught at Princeton and other
American universities and later returned to Italy.

Mann to Kahler

Pacific Palisades
June 14, 1942[1]

Dear friend Kahler:

At last I get around to saying hello to you and to thanking
you. There is always so much to do, and the letter-writing
hours are often taken from me by those who worry very little
about the time of people like us, and then are usually the same
persons who in all innocence wonder *when* we manage to
do "all that."

How kindly you have again remembered my birthday, and
your dear mother too. I must include a page for her. The
sweets and cigars have arrived in good condition. The good
old Optimos! It was a clever thought on your part. They are
very hard to get here, and smoking them, I feel keenly and
nostalgically transported back to the old times when we lived
in the same place. I wonder whether we did right to leave
those days behind us? It remains a question that we answer
one way or the other at different times. The mode of life here
has great advantages, but there is a good deal missing; we

[62]

often feel ourselves "far from cultivated people," are ill informed, and even the famous climate is not entirely salutary. In the long run we sense that the desert air withholds certain elements from us. I don't know what, iodine or calcium or something else that belongs in the body's economy. The absence of it produces a great deal of fatigue, but without promoting sleep at all. I must constantly raise my blood pressure by small doses of thyroid extract to keep myself reasonably alert. But is that right? Should man interfere with his God-given blood pressure?

But we delight daily in the house and garden, and I have already done my study some honor. In spite of regular and irregular interruptions the *Joseph* has advanced almost rapidly. The scene of his revealing himself is already in the past; I am by now lingering over the reunion between father and son, and I only wish I could read some of the chapters aloud to you. Erika laughed herself to tears over a good many passages, and it is true that the element of humor is more and more gaining the upper hand in this volume. It is an epic jest, a comic fairy tale of humanity, and I sometimes think that posterity will wonder how such things could have come into being in our times. Sagging parts are inevitable. The most successful section in this volume is undoubtedly the Tamar episode, some fifty pages long. She provides the book with a distinctive woman character, a fantastic individual who at any cost, and successfully, fits herself into the sacred story and the lineage of David. At the same time the thing remains difficult to the end, and will in fact grow increasingly difficult because more and more new accents, forms, and narrative tricks have to be invented in order to make the familiar suspenseful.

In addition I am busy editing my political essays and speeches of 1923-41.[2] They are to be published now, and I have written a foreword for them. Alas, the translation —

what torment! Unfortunately, I know just about enough English now to feel obliged to look things over. It was much better when I didn't even look.

It fills me with infinite respect to see all that you accomplish and endure and the way you hold up your end. Molly Shenstone[3] wrote us that she had visited you and you had looked tired — which gave me a pang. Rest up well during the summer. I am looking forward eagerly to the book you will be publishing with Kurt Wolff.[4]

Have you read the letters of Verdi,[5] which Bermann and Landshoff[6] have published? First-rate reading, a noble, great life full of dignity. And what political clarity in 1870! "The disaster of France fills my heart with despair ... If it falls, let us not deceive ourselves, all our liberties will fall, and then falls our civilization too. Let our litterateurs and our politicians praise the knowledge and science and even (God forgive them) the art of these victors. But if they would only look a little below the surface, they would see that the old blood of the Goths still flows in their veins, that they are monstrously proud, hard, intolerant, rapacious beyond measure and scornful of everything that is not German. A people of intellect without heart — a strong people, but they have no grace ... *We shall not escape the European war and it will engulf us.*"[7]

Keep well! I hope Fine has risen out of the pit again.[8] And that we will be seeing each other in the autumn!

Yours,
T. M.

1. *Briefwechsel.*
2. *Order of the Day.*
3. In Princeton, Molly Shenstone, the wife of Allen Shenstone, professor of physics, helped with Thomas Mann's correspondence in English from 1938 to 1941.
4. *Man the Measure.* Kurt Wolff (1887-1963), German and American publisher, emigrated to southern France and Italy in 1931, to the

United States in 1941, where he founded Pantheon Books and, subsequently, Helen and Kurt Wolff Books as a division of Harcourt, Brace & World.

5. *Verdi: The Man in His Letters,* ed. and selected by Franz Werfel and Paul Stefan, trans. Edward Downes (New York, 1942).

6. Fritz Landshoff (b. 1901), publisher, left Germany in 1933 and headed the German exiles department of Querido Verlag in Amsterdam. He happened to be visiting England during the German invasion of Holland, went to New York in the winter of 1940, and there joined Gottfried Bermann Fischer in setting up the short-lived American publishing house L. B. Fischer Corporation.

7. Quoted in English in the original.

8. An allusion to Joseph's resurrections.

Kahler to Mann

Princeton
May 9, 1943[1]

My dear Friend:

I found your wonderful Joseph speech[2] here when I came out for the weekend — since the end of March I have been spending the weekdays in New York, where I have been going over the English version of my last chapter[3] with Eleanor Wolff,[4] editing it sentence by sentence in pitched linguistic battles. Your quiet reproach is only too justified, and I am greatly abashed. I had the strongest impulse to tell you how I hailed the completion of the *Joseph*, and how painful it was to me not to have been present on the evening of the day you wrote the last sentence of this opus, the growth of whose later parts I had been privileged to watch from nearby. This book, with its multiple links of intensely personal and universal experience, with its timeless idea and its timely references, and with my shared experience in the circumstances of its development, has grown so close to my heart that I feel my being far away at the time of its completion as a piece of cruelty on the part of fate!

I wanted to tell you all this, and to say it immediately upon hearing of the happy event. But I was so dreadfully weary from work just after the news came — I am unfortunately not so disciplined as you, and my disorganization after a few fruitless days of work paralyzes me so that I can say nothing, let alone the proper festive things that should be said on such an occasion.

But now the lecture, which I immediately read straight through to the end in one breath, so to speak, with the keenest suspense and persistent delight. It has, I think, turned out especially well; it is one of the finest and most suggestive self-interpretations in existence. What a span, from the ego, on through the fathers and "Mothers,"[5] to the mythic future — alas, it's only too mythical, this future! How fine, and how close to me, is your concept of divinity, the idea of the relationship of God and man, and your view of the religious spirit. This lecture is in every respect the counterpart of the introduction; it belongs in all future editions, at the conclusion of the entire work. It closes the circle; it makes contact with the introduction in the present, your own wholly personal present and that of our world.

I shall again postpone any report on myself until my wearisome monster boat is launched at last. I am already heartily sick of the changeling — for that it is surely going to turn out to be, in keeping with circumstances. What are you planning, or what are you already undertaking? Please be generous and once more give me plenty of news of yourself!

Thanks, and all the best to Katia!

Ever yours,
E. K.

P.S. Jakob Burckhardt, *Weltgeschichtliche Betrachtungen,*[6]

[66]

Introduction, 2: "We must lament as the most painful loss of all the impossibility of writing a history of Egypt's intellectual evolution, for at best that could be done only in hypothetical form, as a novel, say"!

1. *Briefwechsel.*

2. "Joseph and His Brothers," presented at the Library of Congress, November 17, 1942 ("The Joseph Novels," trans. Konrad Katzenellenbogen, *Atlantic Monthly,* 171 [February 1943]); in Thomas Mann, *Gesammelte Werke* (12 vols.; Frankfurt, 1960), XI, 654-669.

3. Of *Man the Measure.*

4. Eleanor Wolff (b. 1907), translator, was the coeditor, with Herbert Steiner, of *Erich Kahler* (New York, 1951), a book of homage to Kahler.

5. "Fathers" probably refers to the Hebrew patriarchs, and "Mothers" to the dwellers in the mysterious realm of the Mothers, into which Faust descends in Goethe's *Faust.*

6. 1905 (*Force and Freedom: Reflections on History,* 1943).

Mann to Kahler

Pacific Palisades
May 18, 1943[1]

Dear friend Kahler:

You disproportionately rewarded me with your good letter for the little gift. I am just as much to blame as you for the thinness of our correspondence, and each of us can only say to the other, "But you know how it is." In my case it is that I have a superstitious qualm about writing letters in the mornings; but in the afternoons my secretary comes for dictation only every other day (young Katzenellenbogen,[2] a pleasant fellow with a good English style; unfortunately he will soon be drafted), and on the other day the time is far too often stolen from me by tea-time visitors. I know only to well how you

[67]

have to keep scrambling, and admire such courageous, competent adaptability in a man accustomed to leisure and independence. Your struggles with the translation[3] must be fun, and probably are useful linguistically both to your partner and yourself. So you're in the last chapter! Can it be possible that the book will be out in the fall? I am looking forward to it with the greatest curiosity, and although a Van Loon success[4] is not in prospect, I think it will make a deep impression upon intellectually alive Americans, who do exist. Contemporary experience has, after all, awakened a certain receptivity to such synoptic and daring books. Niebuhr's *The Nature and Destiny of Man*[5] is also a sign of the times.

A deeper reason for our mutual not-writing-much may be the feeling that it is unnecessary. Separated in space, we are on the whole experiencing the same things, and each of us knows fairly precisely what the other is feeling and thinking about them. For example, about the news that American officers in Africa have protested against the playing of the Russian national anthem. (I was assured that this was true.) Or about the news that the Italian *Communists* want to overthrow the dynasty ("Jews and Communists"). Or, on the other hand, about the mad and frightful blow against the German dikes by the R.A.F. [Royal Air Force]. The episode has something symbolic about it; I cannot help thinking that in Germany — if for example the summer offensive in Russia fails — all the dikes will soon give way. Europe will be ours again. I think we may allow ourselves to believe that now, and can even begin to grow accustomed to the idea. For example, everyone is feverishly preparing for the reopening of the German book market. People obviously credit the country with a colossal appetite for books. German books are even being printed in London, I hear. In all haste Bermann persuaded me to renew our contract and, to my enormous surprise, actually put a few thousand dollars on the table — out of sheer terror of the erupting competition. The *Joseph* manuscript has arrived in Stockholm, and together with it new editions of *Zauberberg* [*The Magic Mountain*], *Lotte* [*The Beloved Returns*], and *Die Vertauschten Köpfe* [*The Transposed Heads*] are going into print. Stocking up for "the day," so it seems — or else the Gestapo men in Italy must have bought the books.

We are living our palm and lemon days, with only slight variations. At the moment, and for some time to come, both grandsons[6] from San Francisco are with us, since their mother, the little Swiss girl, has taken a defense job. (She is a tank cleaner.) Having the little folks in the house is amusing, of course, but a nasty burden on my wife, especially since provisioning the household is no longer an easy matter. For me the children are pure pleasure. Anthony (Tonio), nine months, is not a real personality yet. But Frido is the most charming three-year-old I have ever seen, so pretty and roguish that my heart swells when I as much as look at him. He is now beginning to talk with an effort, and rejoices over every word he manages. When he has had enough of something, or wants to console himself because there is no more of it, he says, " 'habt" ["had"]. I find that very good. When I am dying, I too shall say " 'habt." I must definitely write about him. Perhaps I will include him in my next novel. For I find myself willing to give the war time for one more medium-sized novel. It is a kind of modern story of a man who sells his soul to the devil, and a tissue of theology, medicine, music, and politics, for it is to be full of German dolefulness. Incidentally, I cannot guarantee that it will be written. I am just feeling my way around it in reverie.

If only the University of California would at last offer you a professorship! Perhaps when the book is out.

All of us send our regards. Convey them to your mother also.

Yours,
Thomas Mann

[69]

1. *Briefwechsel.*

2. Konrad Kellen (formerly Katzenellenbogen; b. 1913), a friend of Erika and Klaus Mann who emigrated to the United States in 1936, was Thomas Mann's secretary from 1941 to 1943. He became an officer in the American army, worked for Radio Free Europe eleven years, and is the author of *Khrushchev — A Political Portrait* (1961).

3. Of *Man the Measure* from German to English, the language in which it was published.

4. Hendrik Willem Van Loon, *Thomas Jefferson* (New York, 1943). A copy of the book, with a dedication by the author, remains in Thomas Mann's library in the Thomas Mann Archives, Zurich.

5. Reinhold Niebuhr, *The Nature and Destiny of Man* (2 vols.; London and New York, 1941, 1943).

6. The children of Michael and Gret Moser Mann.

Mann to Kahler

Pacific Palisades
December 13, 1943[1]

Dear Kahler:

While the wheels spun[2] I conceived the enclosed little article.[3] Please see to it that it is used as it stands, with the added names. The parallel mention of your book came quite naturally. I both wanted to and had to incude poor Frank,[4] because otherwise he would weep salt tears and complain of disloyalty. Why should such a *statement*[5] in honor of a book not also include other works by another publisher?

With good memories and friendly greetings,

Yours,
Thomas Mann

1. Found by Alice Kahler among her husband's papers; typewritten, so probably dictated.

2. That is, on the train back to Los Angeles. Mann was returning from his long lecture tour, which lasted a full two months between October 9 and December 8, 1943.

3. A statement supporting a fund to be used for the publication of Hermann Broch's *Der Tod des Vergil* in German as well as English. See the next letter.

4. Bruno Frank. The book mentioned was probably Frank's *Die Tochter* (Amsterdam, 1943).

5. This word is in English in the original.

Kahler to Mann

January 5, 1944[1]

Dear Thomas Mann:

Kurt Wolff[2] sent me your letter to him, and took occasion to admit for the first time the request he had touchingly made to you with my interests in mind, although not at all with my assent. You know how hard it has always been for me to enlist others, no matter how close and well-loved friends they may be, in my own behalf, and I have not done it often in my life — my imagination has prevented me. So you may conceive how sorry I am, and pained, to have been the involuntary cause of as much as a moment's anxiety on your part of having your work disturbed, and to have given rise to a few annoyed and uncomfortable hours. Anyone who has ever been really obsessed with a many-layered project understands that craving to get to work, and to do nothing else! The feeling is comparable only to physical thirst. And he knows also the animal fury that flares uncontrollably against anything that detains him from work. Not only would I not like, for anything in the world, to be the cause of such a fury — but also anything useful can be created only when we have clear heads, when we feel an easy willingness, and in fact a stimulus and "exuberance," to get to it.

So do not, in your heart, blame me for it, or Kurt Wolff either. You can imagine how difficult it is for him to establish his truly high-quality publishing house. He is just beginning; his connections with leading journalists are still much too new and tenuous; and although the prestige of the house among connoisseurs and readers is already amazing, given the brief period it has been in existence, it understandably does not yet have the means to compete with the big American houses in the kind of massive publicity that is necessary here. My book[2] is Pantheon's first original publication, and in spite of my warnings Kurt Wolff has placed great hopes in it. He imagined, I think, that it would make a breakthrough to a wider audience for his publishing house as well. So far there is very little sign of that. I have had the misfortune (though I am also at fault because of my slowness) to have my principal books come out in exile. Everywhere I am an unwanted foreigner, without authentic authorization by a native land — alas, I never had any such unequivocal native land. But I have fallen between two stools, not only with respect to countries and groups, but also with respect to the categories by which people are accustomed to classify products of the mind. And so I do not encounter any ready apperception. The intellectual senses necessary to perceive even the problems that concern me don't seem to exist — those problems seem to lie either below or at the threshold of stimulation. No wonder that so far this book is suffering the same fate here as *Der Deutsche Charakter* did in Switzerland. The major newspapers and magazines in New York, Boston, and Washington have as yet made no comment at all, and in the reviews that have appeared I detect a good deal of anxiously embarrassed, vague, lukewarm, empty praise, which I don't care about at all, but not a single really concerned examination, not a single coming to grips with the *subject*, which alone might bring back my work into the general consciousness and obtain for it some real reverberation. Characteristic of this attitude is a remark by the *New York Times* critic (Orville Prescott), whom somebody asked about my book: "We are frightened by this book, we are simply out of our depth." The only review so far that really gave me pleasure was a vicious attack in the *Daily Mirror,* which scented a "fellow traveller" in me.[3]

Oh well, all this is no surprise to me. I was prepared for it and must bear it. But Kurt Wolff feels it with bitter concern; and it is only to explain and to apologize for his conduct that I have expatiated to you on this disagreeable state of affairs.

I hope and trust that meanwhile you are once more immersed in your magnificent enterprise.[4] It fascinates me, and I am following its progress with the greatest suspense and good wishes, and sharing your fears for it as well. Please let me know from time to time how it is going! I'd like very much to read your Moses[5] story — is there, by any chance, an old copy you can spare? There's little point in my buying the book, since your contribution is the only thing in it that interests me. Also I much prefer to read you in German.

I have received your statement for Broch — unfortunately it will not be possible to use it with the inclusion of the other names. I think I did not express myself clearly: Your statement is intended for a circular, to be sent out privately, containing a special recommendation of the *Vergil*[6] and inviting subscriptions. From the other statements, which K. W. [Kurt Wolff] will send you, you will see that a reference to other books will not fit into this context. It has nothing to do with the fact that Bruno Frank's book[7] was brought out by another publisher — my name, too, must not figure in the circular, which is meant to serve exclusively the purpose of the subscription. I must therefore ask for your authorization that only the passage referring to Broch be used. K. W. and Broch will also do this separately.

Unfortunately I saw the Borgeses only once in New York; his sudden kidney stone and our Princeton grippes prevented us from meeting. It was very sad, and a great pity. At any rate I saw Gogoi[8] for the first time in the company of her new tropical beauty of a nanny. Both made a great impression on me. I'm sorry to say I again thought Medi rather too thin and pale — a slender thing who seems overburdened by her new pregnancy. She was dear as ever. Borgese was bursting with keen sarcasms. His book,[9] incidentally, is very brilliant, full of trenchant formulations — although I find I cannot agree with a good deal of it.

I had a letter from Golo from which I gather that he is slated for some overseas assignment, which worries me greatly. Couldn't something be done to keep him from that? He has gone through enough, and would accomplish more important, less replaceable things at the desk or on the lecture platform. You know he isn't the type for intelligence service, where what counts is great agility either in the line of journalism or in political psychology. And on the other hand he is one of the few whom I — quite aside from all personal feelings — would unequivocally want to see spared for the great postwar tasks. You yourself certainly cannot exert any influence, but isn't there some confidential go-between who could do something to this effect? Here I have seen similar interventions succeed. That Gentz[10] has at last found a good publisher was a great pleasure to me.

Yours,
E. K.

May I softly remind you of *Richter*.[11]

1. *Briefwechsel.*
2. *Man the Measure.*
3. The quotations are in English in the original.
4. *Doktor Faustus*: *Das Leben des deutschen Tonsetzers Adrian Leverkühn, erzählt von einem Freunde* (Stockholm, 1947; *Doctor Faustus*: *The Life of the German Composer Adrian Leverkühn as Told by a Friend* [1948]).

[74]

5. *The Tables of the Law,* a novella Mann wrote for *The Ten Commandments: Ten Novels of Hitler's War against the Moral Code,* ed. Armin L. Robinson (New York, 1943), an anthology in which each story deals with one of the Ten Commandments and its violation by Hitler.

6. Hermann Broch, *Der Tod des Vergil* (*The Death of Virgil* [New York, 1945]), written during the seven years he lived with the Kahlers in Princeton. The metrical translations of the extensive quotations from the *Aeneid* are by Erich Kahler. Hermann Broch (1886-1951), the Austrian novelist, dramatist, and literary critic left Vienna in 1938 and became a resident of the United States. Among his other novels are *The Sleepwalkers* (1931-1932) and *The Unknown Quantity* (1935). Kahler edited Broch's poems (*Gedichte* [Zurich, 1953]) and wrote *Die Philosophie von Hermann Broch* (Tübingen, 1962).

7. *Die Tochter.*

8. Angelica Borgese, the daughter of Elisabeth Mann Borgese and G. A. Borgese, born December 30, 1940.

9. *Common Cause* (New York, 1943).

10. Golo Mann's *Secretary of Europe: The Life of Friedrich Gentz, Enemy of Napoleon* (New Haven: Yale University Press, 1946) (*Friedrich von Gentz:Geschichte eines europäischen Staatsmannes* [Zurich, 1947]).

11. Werner Richter (1888-1969), historian and journalist (*Berliner Tageblatt*), went into exile in 1936, first to Italy, then to Switzerland, in 1941 to the United States. He returned to Switzerland (Massagno) after World War II. He was the author of popular biographies of Emperor Friedrich III (1938), Ludwig II (1939), Crown Prince Rudolf of Austria (1941), George Washington (1946), Bismarck (1962).

Mann to Kahler

Pacific Palisades
January 16, 1944[1]

Dear, good Friend:

You have written so kindly and understandingly, making me feel so much better despite my chagrin at being so behind-hand, that I can do nothing but thank you. I suppose it is a natural and inevitable chagrin: I am simply beginning to feel my years, the years of an already long life that was strained and precarious from early on. Between you and me, I am often totally *tired out,* quite *lazy.* I find myself dreading demands on my energies that I formerly took as a matter of course. A habitual urge to work has been concentrated in the morning hours (old Haydn: "When I have had a little breakfast I sit down to compose." The good fellow!). By afternoon I really no longer feel like doing anything. I uneasily anticipate the secretary's coming so that I can dictate letters, and repeatedly find that whatever I force myself to undertake at this time of day turns out badly, so that I realize I shall have to free one or two mornings for such tasks.

I admit, it has always been more or less that way. But a distinct tendency to take it easy and a growing inclination to evade additional strains are nevertheless apparent. Still and all, I have not yet neglected very much, or essential matters; and in the case of your book I can honestly say that the delay has at the moment purely superficial reasons. I was unable to take the volume with me; along with many others, it could not be stowed into our baggage. A small library with, heaven help us, even manuscripts included had accumulated in our hotel room. We gave it to Bermann for mailing, and this package has incomprehensibly not yet arrived. For a while the Christmas-mail turmoil made its nonappearance excusable; but by now the matter has long since stopped being a joke, and we have twice complained to Bermann about it. He has been rather remiss in other matters also. I have had to apologize to several people about his failing to make any comment about their manuscripts, or failing to return them. If I had the book in my hands again, a short essay on it would undoubtedly come about of its own accord, as a response from within. Everything you tell me about the weak and timorous reception it has encountered makes me determined to speak up for it; and only yesterday this determination was quickened by a conversation with Erwin Kalser,[2] when we met at a party and who proved to be deeply stirred by the book. For days, he said, he had been unable to put it down.

I cannot tell you how grateful I am to you for your keen interest in my new narrative experiment. It is moving forward again, although much more slowly than in the first flush of novelty before the tour. If I were to neglect that, it would be really bad. But with patience, care, circumspection, and getting up on time it will take form, after "a little breakfast." After lectures I have repeatedly had my attention called to the arc which allegedly leads from old *Buddenbrooks* to it. And it is a curious coincidence that just at this time a good many individuals, independently of one another, have reread that forty-four-year-old first novel with amazing pleasure. The Franks have done so, and almost at the same time Werfel,[3] deathly ill, asked me for a copy of the book and at my last visit spoke of it with unqualified enthusiasm: "An immortal masterpiece, indestructible!" He said it struck him as altogether strange to see the empirical person of the author standing at his bedside this way. Those happy youthful efforts undertaken at just the favorable moment can be an equivocal blessing. Sometimes all a man can subsequently do is to fill out the remainder of his life, possibly a long remainder, in a tolerably dignified fashion, while always being the man of that first work — the more so the longer he lives. I shouldn't want to think of *Buddenbrooks* in terms of the *Cavalleria rusticana.* But perhaps it is possible to think of it in terms of *Der Freischütz,* which was a real, at least a German, event. Oh well, *Oberon* and *Euryanthe* are still in the repertory ... And after all I do think I managed to shape my later life more in the Goethean pattern.

The Moses story is being well received, and of course it is

always consoling to hear that you've done something good *only recently*. But you're right not to ask for the book. I am very much afraid that my contribution is far and away the best. Some of the others are actually ridiculous and compromising, for example a description of Copenhagen by Rebecca West[4] so ignorant that people in Europe will hold their sides. More's the pity. Unfortunately I have only the manuscript of the Moses original. Couldn't you get a copy from Bermann Fischer?

We talk about you often, and wish you were here. I keep thinking the day will come when you will belong to us again.

Warmly,

> Yours,
> Thomas Mann

The questions about what should be done with Germany after the victory come in an unending stream. I do not say a word. If you urge leniency, you may be dreadfully disavowed by the Germans. If you urge stringency, you fall into a wrong and unconscionable position toward the country whose language you write. Moreover, all discussions about the bear's skin[5] still seem to me weirdly premature.

We have completed our citizenship examination, and so are actually *cives romani*. But I imagine we will be better advised to travel to Europe on a Czech passport.

1. *Briefwechsel.*

2. Dr. Erwin Kalser (1883-1958), actor, emigrated to Zurich in 1933, to the United States in 1939, and after the war returned to Zurich, then to Berlin.

3. Franz Werfel (1890-1945), the expressionist poet, novelist, and dramatist, who was born in Prague, left Vienna in 1940 and came to the United States. Among his works are *The Forty Days of Musa Dagh* (1934) and *The Song of Bernadette* (1942).

4. Rebecca West (pseudonym of Cicely Fairfield, b. 1892), British journalist, novelist, and critic, had contributed a story, "Thou Shalt

Not Make Any Graven Image," to *The Ten Commandments*.

5. An allusion to the old joke that you had better kill your bear before you think about what to do with its skin.

Kahler to Mann

Dear Friend:

Praise be to birthdays! They are a firm date, a deadline to endless postponements. I think almost half a year has passed since I last heard directly from you or that, it seems to me, I wrote to you or Katia. Golo told us a little before he disappeared all too suddenly, and I learned from Mrs. Lowe[2] that the *Faust* has made rapid progress and that she will soon be receiving more manuscript after all . . . Whenever I think of it, I begin longing to know how it's faring, how you have done it and structured it, and what else you may have been doing along the way. How many episodes I could anticipate at the time you told me the story, how many flowery and peppery opportunities — my God, or rather, my devil! And this time what a justification you have to seize upon every occasion in this terrific book, for so it promises to be. And so I am licking my lips — and probably will have to go on doing so until the fall, *hélas,* when you return.

I shall scarcely be able to get away from here, or at most for a week, because of my mother and the problems connected with her health, at the moment somewhat stabilized but still extremely precarious, and the difficulty of caring for her. And yet I could well use a change, after three uninterrupted years in Princeton and given the state of veritable gloom I am in. Ah, how good it would be not to have to think, not to have to know, not to have to foresee anything. To go off into the bush a bit, just for a little while, by the sea, in the woods, as long as they are still there.

Do you know what is hardest to bear in the era that is advancing upon us, and especially in this country? It is this omnipresent, terrifying feeling of futility! Not only are natural law, the elements, absolute truth all gone — the same thing is taking place in the purely physical, animal condition. We've known all that for a long time, thought and written about it, but we haven't entirely believed it physically, believed it with the naïve base of the body. We've counted on saving ourselves romantically somewhere, in the existence of nature, in the primeval forests somewhere in the world. But that hope is being thoroughly crushed. There is not going to be any way out. Nothing for it; back to the human mess, politics, economy, Big Three,[3] Standard Oil, State Dept., Churchill, the pope, and all that follows. What is good old Nature, what are the primeval forest? Bomb fodder. And what primeval forests are left? In the South Sea Islands, where not so long ago the subtle psychological fables of Joseph Conrad were still possible, the Rockette girls[4] are kicking up their legs; and Frank Sinatra[5] will soon be teaching the parrots to sing. No, nature has no permanence; people have won, are continuing to win, and it is becoming impossible to see what for.

Forgive me, my friend, this is hardly in the birthday spirit, and I shouldn't be letting it spill out. But this is me at the moment — if I am to communicate anything truthful from myself, this is what it must be.

Please write again, a few comforting words. Is it true you are doing a film? The newspapers say so. I also read what you published in the *Atlantic* on Germany[6] . . . I have likewise had to comment on this dismal theme, more elaborately than I liked.[7]

I shall think of you on June 6 with the most heartfelt good wishes. The whole household sends regards to you and Katia.

Ever yours,
E. K.

1. *Briefwechsel.*

2. Helen Lowe-Porter.

3. The United States, Russia, and England.

4. The Rockettes, dancers at the Radio City Music Hall, in New York City.

5. Frank Sinatra (b. 1917), American film actor and singer of popular songs.

6. "What Is German?" *Atlantic Monthly,* May 1944.

7. "The German Problem," *Contemporary Jewish Record,* 5 (October 1944).

Mann to Kahler

Pacific Palisades
June 20, 1944[1]

Dear friend Kahler:

My thanks for your kind and thoughtful remembrance of my birthday — a perfectly ordinary sixty-ninth — is long overdue. Soon afterward I had an unpleasant and wearing attack of *intestinal troubles,* which is going the rounds here now, a kind of stomach and intestinal grippe accompanied by much pain and nausea. Just today, when I am at last being permitted to eat a little white meat, Katia is beginning to come down with the same trouble; and it would be bad if she developed a severe case. For without me things go along, but not without her.

Once again, then, your letter was a very welcome gift. Your pessimism, your melancholia, your resignation have too much intelligence behind them to exert a depressing effect; and God knows there is reason for such feelings — although I think that your overlong confinement within venerable Princeton is somewhat affecting your attitude. Forever being with the same professors. The life there soon began to feel constricted to me. I enjoy the distances here — although they

[81]

cost a great deal of gasoline[2] — and the sea wind. At the present time, moreover, associating with musicians is doing me nothing but good. Stravinsky, Schoenberg, Toch, Rubinstein[3] — everybody is here, you know. And then seeing Leonhard Frank,[4] fundamentally a homesick German, dreaming and writing about seventeenth-century Würzburg and the craftsmen of bygone days. He has a remarkable instinct for the secrets of my novel, and often comes to visit. The fact that we don't have you, dear friend, this living-hopelessly-far-away-from-you, which we did not imagine as so permanent and separating, is a constant *crève-coeur*, believe me. We have constantly been tempted to try to secure a professorship for you here, but have refrained, partly because of the difficulty, partly because we know that for the time being you cannot move about freely, and then too because of our sense of the temporariness of all conditions and the possibility of rapid changes.

What will you do when Europe is open? Won't you be drawn back to it after all? To France say, to Prague, Vienna? Since I was unable to imagine the invasion across the Channel and it has nevertheless come off with comparatively few casualties, perhaps I also have exaggerated notions of the enormous difficulties still involved in the conquest of France. The war *may* be rapidly approaching its end. But even if the Germans prove, by fighting to the last cartridge, that they are attached to National Socialism as no other nation is to its regime, that theirs is the most legitimately democratic government of all, it is hard to imagine that the European war will continue beyond the spring of 1945. I rarely think beyond its end, that is, beyond the end of the filthy nonsense that drove us out of Germany. For the past eleven years I have been living for that moment, and do not much worry about what may come afterward. I suppose it's because of my age that I am inclined to think and say: That's your problem! But I should like to depart this life reassured that although all sorts of dubious literary products are possible on the planet whose fleeting acquaintanceship we have made, the greatest stupidity and baseness could after all not last longer than eleven years.

What is this? My hand already feels numb, or rather my head — writing itself is getting to be to much for me. I ought to leave the letter for the time being, to try to make a little something of it later; but I'd rather write again soon. It's time you received your thanks.

We had a joint cable from London from Erika and Golo. Klaus writes from Italy to say he is very satisfied with his work, but that he is eager to get to England so that he can participate in the invasion. It is really what Hofrat Behrens called Joachim's *Biereifer* [excess of zeal].[5] Very worthy, but especially when I think of my wife I can only pray that in the mess we do not lose any of our children.

The San Francisco family are coming for a longish stay next month, and I am looking forward to handsome Fridolin, who they tell us speaks a great deal of English and German. Then the Borgeses will be coming in September and staying over Christmas.

The novel has made marked — to avoid saying "good" — progress. There are already 300 pages, about half.[6] How glad I would be to read some aloud to you!

In three days, on the 23d, we shall be citizens. Curious, curious.

Make the best of this, and warm regards!

Yours,

Thomas Mann

1. *Briefwechsel.*
2. A reference to the wartime rationing of gasoline.
3. Igor Stravinsky (1882-1971), Russian-born conductor and composer, had emigrated from France to the United States. Arnold Schoenberg (1874-1951), Austrian composer and theoretician of music

who created the twelve-tone technique, had come to the United States in 1933. He and Thomas Mann became close friends in California. Subsequently, Schoenberg accused Mann of appropriating his intellectual property by including the twelve-tone technique in *Doctor Faustus,* but was eventually mollified. Ernst Toch (1887-1964), Austrian composer who combined traditional, romantic elements with elements of the New Music, had emigrated to the United States in 1935. Artur Rubinstein (b. 1887), Polish-born pianist, toured extensively in the United States, where he resided during the war. He later returned to France.

4. Leonhard Frank (1882-1961), writer, was an ardent pacifist who went into voluntary exile in 1933. His autobiography, *Links, wo das Herz ist,* was published in 1952.

5. Hofrat Behrens is the medical director of the sanatorium in *The Magic Mountain.* His patient Joachim is the cousin of Hans Castorp, the "hero" of the novel.

6. Thomas Mann was then working on chapter xix of *Doctor Faustus.*

Mann to Kahler

July 28, 1944[1]

Dear friend Kahler:

I only wanted to tell you that the Moses story, which you touchingly ordered, has not yet been published. I saw the proofs only recently, and it will certainly take a few weeks before the book is manufactured. So don't fret! The German *Joseph,*[2] however, is now out, and you are not to buy that, as I scarcely need to say, I think. One of the copies I ordered from Bermann, which should be along any day now, is naturally intended for you.

I was very happy to hear about the forthcoming translations of *Man the Measure.* Haven't you also considered preparing a *German* edition of that? It is absolutely and precisely a book for postwar Europe, and might play a fundamental, purifying, central part there, especially in *French.*[3]

[84]

I can certainly join with you in telling a story or two of the immaturity, to put it mildly, of American criticism. This last volume of *Joseph,* of all things, a humorous book in a totally popular vein, is represented as a monstrosity overladen with demanding and at the same time inept philosophy full of unbearably Olympian attitudinizing. Idiots.

You surely did not receive my letter in which I thanked you so warmly for yours on my birthday. The situation with the mail is discouraging. I hope you do not imagine that I would have passed over in silence your friendly congratulations.

In all probability we shall be coming in January. Hard to see far ahead these days, but it is probable.

Yours,
Thomas Mann

1. Princeton.
2. *Joseph, der Ernährer (Joseph the Provider).*
3. *Man the Measure* has not been published in German or French. A Spanish translation, *Historia universal del hombre* (Mexico City, 1946), had its sixth printing in 1973.

Kahler to Mann

October 10, 1944[1]

My dear Friend:

It is very bad. The blame rests entirely upon me. Everything has arrived safely. Your letter and the *Joseph.* And only my accumulated sincere gratitude is shamefully and disgracefully unpunctual as always. For I wanted to read the *Joseph* before writing. And I am a slow-gaited, pedestrian reader, not one, where I am really involved, to tear through and glance at. Besides, I like to stalk my own game along the way, taking side trips into my private worlds — and God knows this book provides more than enough occasions for doing so. In addition I was unable, as I'd planned, to read on vacation, but had to do so between continual frenzies of work and while thoroughly exhausted by the rigors of this truly sadistic climate. Anyhow, out of the accumulation of such reasons it is October once more, a month that in general I am very fond of because it usually brought you in addition to delicate and golden weather. How pleasant it would have been to *talk* about the *Joseph*. But now that is out, and so it has to be set down on dismal paper.

Well then, I enormously enjoyed this volume, found it light, easygoing, amusing in the highest and profoundest way. More fluid and more purely narrative because the premises have, of course, all been laid down, are familiar and easily handled. I was again struck by the way your kind of ironic multilevel method and delightful, lighthearted digressiveness was predestined to bring close to us the metaphysical cere-moniousness and the many planes of myth in the life of these early peoples, to condense all that into an element of our dailiness, an atmosphere we can almost taste and smell. You *had to* hit upon this world. And it is easy to feel your masterful pleasure in moving within it. Who else could have made it so sensuously tangible?

Apart from all delight, I have again learned a tremendous amount from this book. Above all the fundamental under-standing, enhanced by our very distance, of our nearness to that history. We are permeated by that history which legend has exaggerated beyond proportion and scholarship mum-mified. I say nothing of the wealth of charming references, linguistic, mythic, ethical. The high points, as I see them, are the wonderful dialogue with Amenophis, Tamar, the brothers in Egypt, and Jacob's death.

These innocents here, these "tâm"-less[2] people who "know

not how to live," habitually criticize as inadequacies things that were of the profoundest, most meaningful intention. Hence that business about your "pomposity" and similar charges when they were bothered by your lack of accord with their literary stereotypes. Very well, that can still be viewed as misunderstanding. But their grumbling over the "philosophy" in this gracefully flowing narrative can only be traced to their inveterate dislike of any kind of deeper meaning in general. What will be the fate of *Doctor Faust* when that comes along? Well, you can afford to be wholly indifferent to it. Sufficient unto the day!

As for me, I am thoroughly exhausted. I have had no vacation, that is no change of scene, for three years, and feel it intensely. I had promised Broch to go over the last version of his *Vergil* with him. We thought it would be a matter of two weeks, but it has expanded into a labor of more than two months, the months of the worst summer I have experienced in this country. On top of that came the revision of the translation of Golo's book. That work is still far from complete. It gives me a great deal of pleasure, but requires considerable care and therefore time. His translator is a charming, eccentric old gentleman, a cancer researcher who makes a hobby of languages.[3] I spend many day and night hours with him at the Columbia Club in New York, engaging in lengthy discussions of specific terms and linguistic comparisons. What with all this, my own work moves along very slowly.

In connection with the Gentz book I discovered that we find the German of the Romantics hard to take nowadays. Between the Nazi drivel and what English was taught us, we can no longer appreciate the scintillating vagueness and the foamy, boneless quality of their language.

Please do not punish me for my sluggishness in writing, and let me hear from you about your progress on your *Faust*,[4] which has not ceased to be of burning interest to me. I'd also like to know when we may expect all of you here. I don't imagine anything will come of the trip to Europe so very soon! That will all drag on for quite a while yet.

All the best to Katia, and thanks for your highly appreciated letter. And special regards to the Borgeses, who have also fallen silent. The Italians' manifesto was heartwarming![5] Everyone here in the household sends greetings and regards.

Ever yours,
Erich Kahler

1. *Briefwechsel.*

2. *Tâm* is a Hebrew word used frequently in *Joseph and His Brothers.* "Of Jacob it had always been said that he was *'tam,'* meaning that he was upright, and dwelt in tents. But *tam* is an equivocal word, not properly rendered by 'upright.' It is both positive and negative, it is yes and no, light and darkness, life and death" (*Joseph the Provider* [New York, 1944], p. 258).

3. *Secretary of Europe,* trans. William H. Woglom.

4. The narrative in *Faustus* is a variation on the Faust legend; the composer Adrian Leverkühn makes a pact with the devil.

5. Perhaps the first open, published demand — September 21, 1944, by Pietro Nenni, then secretary-general of the Italian Socialist Party — that the Allied Control Commission leave the country and permit Italians to "administer [their] misery alone"; or the acceptance by the government ministers of Premier Ivanoe Bonomi's plea for unity, September 26.

Mann to Kahler

1550 San Remo Drive
Pacific Palisades, California
October 20, 1944[1]

Dear, good Friend:

You have written so finely and helpfully about the *Joseph* — and I have been reproaching myself for putting you through this. A book of this sort is a Greek gift, of course. First one has to read the thing. At best that can afford some entertainment for certain stretches, but in the press of daily affairs it is hard to get done. And then the reader has to write something good and significant to an author greedy for his Vitamin P(raise) — one burden more on top of others. Long since I had been upbraiding myself for not having said to you. "Don't write to me; we'll talk about it in the winter!" And now I cannot help being glad after all that I culpably neglected to forbid comment. For a letter like yours is naturally a great delight, a comfort and tonic and gives one hope that — since after all it isn't so long ago that I did something so very good — the work I happen to be engaged on at the moment will also turn out to be not entirely foolish stuff. "Your progress on your *Faust*"! How that sounds! As if Zelter or Humboldt were writing to Weimar.[2] I really chuckled to myself. But there is something attractively mythic about such a remark, and all halfway good German books have much of *Faust* in them — *The Magic Mountain* and *Joseph,* less admittedly, also had a good deal of it. This time I come right out with the name — and at the same time try to blur the matter somewhat by the Latin ending of the name: *Doctor Faustus*: *The Life of the German Composer Adrian Leverkühn, as Told by a Friend.* That is the title, as it now stands, and I rather think it does not suggest syphilitic megalomania. The word "German" has crept in willy-nilly, as a symbol of all the sorrows and all the pain of loneliness with which the book deals, and which it itself symbolizes. Something very curious: a kind of melancholic nationalism seems to be erupting in our literature. It represents an entirely new nuance. *Leonhard* Frank, who occasionally reads aloud to us from a new and very talented story set in an old German, small-town, artisan sphere, actually wants to title his work "A German Story."[3] Between you and me, this story is already influenced by the "Germanism" of my novel, which for that very reason transports him every time I read it aloud. — Yes, yes, very strange. All the stranger since my *dégoût* for everything German is growing enormously just now. An impossible, a hopeless race, truly *une race maudite*. They have learned nothing, understand nothing, regret nothing, have not the slightest sense that after all the harm they have done the pose of heroism does not become them, and that their sacred German soil long ago ceased to be sacred and has instead been desecrated again and again by injustice and the utmost baseness. But alongside Hitler and Himmler[4] they will stupidly and uncritically go on defending it with the "fanaticism" that has been drilled into them. It is pitiable, and enough to drive one to despair. Golo read in the *Basler Nationalzeitung* that Frau Elsa Bruckmann (Princess Cartacuzène)[5] attended the Lucerne festival. She curses the Americans fearfully; they deliberately and systematically bomb German children's hospitals. Some persons expressed mild doubt and incidentally asked even more mildly about the dreadful mass killings of children by the Germans. "But you cannot compare that," she replied. "Those were Jewish children." The newspaper adds that it has probably been a mistake to believe that only the *young* Germans were bestialized, and asks what possible hope there is for the future. — The collapse will be purely superficial, and there will never be a surrender. We still don't know what happens when a nation of seventy millions simply refuses to accept its defeat. It is most uncanny.

Warmest regards and all the best!

Yours,
T. M.

P.S. I have a request: old *Julius Bab* (14 Jessica Place, Roslyn Heights, L.I., New York) is supposed to write an article on *Joseph* for the good *Deutsche Blätter* in Santiago de Chile,[6] but cannot obtain a copy from Bermann because the small edition is out of print. Would you be so good as to lend him your copy for two weeks?

1. Princeton.

2. Karl Friedrich Zelter (1758-1832), German music director and composer who set poems by Goethe and Schiller to music, engaged in an extensive correspondence with Goethe, who was at the court of Weimar. Wilhelm von Humboldt (1767-1835), German philologist and diplomat, was a great liberal reformer and a friend of Goethe.

3. *The Baroness* (London, 1950); *Deutsche Novelle* (Munich, 1954).

4. Heinrich Himmler (1900-1945) was chief of the Gestapo and all German police forces, 1936-1945. In 1945 he committed suicide after his capture by the British.

5. Elsa Bruckmann, née Princess Cartacuzène, was the wife of the Munich publisher Hugo Bruckmann.

6. "Thomas Mann's 'Joseph und seine Brüder,' " *Deutsche Blätter,* September–October 1945. Julius Bab (1880-1955), a noted critic, left Germany in 1933.

Kahler to Mann

Princeton
December 17, 1944[1]

My dear ones,

Quickly, before the year runs out — already another year, alas! — and before you all, I hope, come rushing here, to my great joy, I want to pay my epistolary debts and send you one grand summary thanks for all the good things, the important things, the thoroughly savored things that have come in your letters, and also for the truly delightful picture,[2] which has evoked and held the full charm of characters and ages — it is going to be framed and hung on the wall.

I shall save for face-to-face communication all the many matters that have accumulated through the year. For now, nothing but good wishes, the kind that cannot be telegraphed. Merry Christmas! And may the important next year be productive, full of success! For a moment let us forget the world, which is particularly ghastly.

Bon voyage, and looking forward to seeing you soon,

Yours,

Erich Kahler

Regards and good wishes from the whole household!

[*The following letter from Hermann Broch was enclosed with Kahler's letter.*]

One Evelyn Place
Princeton, New Jersey
December 18, 1944

My dear Dr. Mann:

Fate would have it that this letter has turned into Christmas greeting — it went unwritten by stages, first after reading the glorious fourth [volume of] *Joseph,* then in connection with the unspeakable attacks on you, which, however, you have now dealt with in a way that could not have been better and finer.[3]

I became intensely preoccupied — how could I help it? — with the fourth volume. To the extent that I can venture upon the great theme, I should like to seal my exit from literature, as once I did my entry into it, with an essay on Thomas Mann, showing that the evolution which lies between *Death in Venice* and *Joseph* is nothing less than the development of the *Zeitgeist* and its potentialities for artistic expression. As far as I can recall, as far back as 1912 I correctly divined in *Death in Venice* the renunciation of bourgeois expression and therefore of the novel itself. And although you have retained the novel form, it is clear to me that you have put on a magnificent and inimitable display of farewell fireworks. What is more, they are already being aimed into new territory. I need not say with what suspense I am looking forward to your *Faust*. You call the book a "dangerous enterprise," so it is one that penetrates even further into new territory, once again to set up there a mirror of the spirit and spirits of the period of its genesis.

You make my decision to abandon literary writing, or rather my abiding by this decision, at once both easy and hard. Easy because I have a pretty good sense of distances and know that the bold leaps of the mind, which for you represent the natural extension of a great and consistent lifework, cannot be matched by anyone. But hard, because the new territory you reveal exerts a constant temptation. But the *Vergil* taught me my limits; the revision for printing took a full eight months instead of the eight weeks I had foreseen; and although it can all be rated as objectively correct, in the background was the feeling of having gone astray into unpredictable immensities, into a realm in which the equilibrium between expression and the world is abolished and the work no longer has any source of legitimacy. Since the world has become overpowering to man, the possibility of literary expression has also come to an end. This is the break in the line of development. The road from Cervantes to Tolstoy is shorter than that from Tolstoy to you (or — after a fork — to Joyce). For the boundary of expression has just been crossed.

But beyond every boundary there begins, to repeat, new territory; and the world, too, is in a boundary situation today. At the moment it does not look very pretty, neither politically nor militarily; no one can say how long the horror will go on, and the longer it lasts the more devastating the psychological and hence the political consequences will be, the more civility and civilization will be excluded from the shaping of the world. So far the young people who come back from over there (to the extent that I have come to know them) are still amazingly sound, above all full of contempt for the lack of seriousness they find here (the letters of my son, too, who is probably in the Balkans now, show amazing insight). But this is valid only for the moment, and they represent only a small cross section. I hope that my work on mass psychology,[4] to which I have at last been able to return, will provide a few halfway valid insights into the relationships, and in addition I hope that there will be some way to put these findings to practical use. For despite the present gloom, the psychological data suggest — insofar as they are correct — that we may count on the dawning of another humane period for mankind. I should only like to witness it, and I resent the brevity of human life.

But Christmas and New Year's permit *wishful thinking.* And so let me wish you and your wife, and so all of us, a pleasant 1945; your visit in the East will in any case start it off pleasantly for everyone. I kiss your ladies' hands, and with cordial regards am

Sincerely yours,
Hermann Broch

1. *Briefwechsel.*

2. Of Thomas Mann with his two young grandsons, the children of Michael and Gret Mann.

3. Mann's article "What Is German?" *Atlantic Monthly,* May 1944, attempted to explain the presence in the German national character of laudable as well as ruinous features. Mann was attacked because the article was interpreted as advocating a soft peace. To an attack in the July issue by Henri Peyre, professor of French at Yale, Mann replied with an article, "In My Defense," in the December issue.

4. *Massenpsychologie*: *Schriften aus dem Nachlass* (Zurich, 1959).

Mann to Kahler

Pacific Palisades
December 23, 1944[1]

Dear, good friend Kahler:

The letters from both of you have just arrived — please give Hermann Broch my warm thanks for his weighty and elegant letter, which gives me such a lift. Would that there were some truth to his picture of me. At any rate what he says shows considerable insight into the general situation; and in fact I have sometimes ventured to regard Joyce as a playmate, although also as an antagonist; for I am a decided traditionalist, even though I have often had my fun with the old forms and have — reverently — taken liberties with them.

Broch can rest assured that in his *Vergil* he has created a significant monument of the times, and one that is totally unique. I am looking forward with intense interest to his *Massenpsychologie,* and am convinced that he is producing a textbook for the world that may bring about and prevent a good many things.

Your letter, dear friend, with its rejoicing in a near reunion, made us realize how much at fault we have been for having failed to let you know that we have had to postpone this trip. Everybody knows except you; we ought to have written you long ago. I have been distinctly unwell: an intestinal grippe, bad enough in itself and with a postlude of a very painful infection of the facial nerve (trigeminus). I was in such poor shape that I could not dream of traveling in January, into the cold, and have still not really recovered my strength. I cancelled the lecture tour, but reserved the possibility of making it up in much shortened form some time during the spring. At the moment I am thinking of March. But now the Library of Congress wants to avail itself of this necessary postponement by turning my lecture there into a kind of birthday celebration. They insist that I speak there on the day itself if at all possible, but in any case shift my visit so that it is close to the June date. I must make that concession to the library, and do so gladly, in the first place because of the kind intention behind the request, and then in view of the pleasant season, and finally because this arrangement gives me more time to write away at the novel before I have to compose the lecture. It is to deal with Germany and the Germans, you know, and you can imagine that I am in no hurry to start on that subject.[2] So in all likelihood it will be May, the early or middle part of the month, before we set out on our trip. Are you very disappointed? We are too, from one point of view. But the postponement also has its good side.

Yesterday a surprising call from Erika from New York, where she had arrived on a troop transport ship! Thank God. I was secretly worried about her, for you never knew where she might be knocking around, possibly within the zone of the German offensive. It's a fine mess, and has probably prolonged the war by a year or so. Do you think there is any chance the Nazis might, even now, ultimately wear us down and obtain a peace for *themselves?* I suppose that couldn't happen after all.

Merry Xmas to you personally and to your loved ones, and a good new year!

Yours,
Thomas Mann

1. *Briefwechsel.*
2. "Germany and the Germans," presented May 29, 1945.

Kahler to Mann

My dear Friend:

The shame of my not writing reeks to heaven; even repeatedly mentioning it has become bothersome, and so I pass
quickly over it. But these days, when so many things are
happening and are about to happen that have long been
awaited, hoped for, and feared, we must send a greeting to
each other. An entire shared period of life is just ending for
us, a period of shared experience, suffering, and knowledge.
What we knew when nobody wanted to believe it, neither
on this side of the water nor the other, now lies exposed —
not only the stench and filth on which the pseudo triumphs of
the past decade were erected, but also the whole truly
apocalyptic tragedy of the German people and this era of ours.
All the embitterment, in fact all deeper interest in the denouement of the Nazi monstrosity, had somehow faded away
for me in recent weeks. Isn't it the same with you? Our most
insistent thoughts and anxieties were already far into the
postwar period. But now that Germany lies exposed, it has
all come back; all of it, back from the deepest past, is suddenly
present again and occupies one's whole mind, one's thoughts
and feelings. I keep coming around to it: What are the Nazis?
A symptom, miserable instruments of a judgment, unsuspect-
ing, blind self-scourgers — and not only a scourge of the
Germans themselves, I must insist, but of our entire age. What
an astonishing turn things take — things we had long ago painfully thought out down to the details, had anticipated in our
imaginations — but the real happening carries us along like
the rapids of a river into wholly new imports and prospects.
Suddenly we are standing where we had so long conceived
ourselves as standing, and an entirely new landscape opens

[97]

up — a frightful landscape, frightful to great distances. To absorb, to digest what that means for our whole human condition, will be the staggering and almost impossible task for the rest of our lifetimes.

Enough, enough. All that does not fit into a letter. I can hardly wait to see you. When will it be? Right in the midst of my tumult of thinking and the commotion of people I am secretly living with your *Faust* manuscript, which I — and here *you* are to blame — illegally, without your permission, have been borrowing from Mrs. Lowe in pieces so I could read it. But you know how strong my feelings of suspense are, and how I tremble for the future of the book!

But we will soon be talking about all that — also about our dear FDR[2], for whom I wept and whom I miss like a true father of the country, or rather, like a roof overhead — but who in the future will perhaps lead his country better from the other side than he would have been able to here on earth, and who therefore died at a brilliantly chosen moment.

Please let me know in good time when you will be arriving. Until then all the best to you and Katia!

Ever yours,
E. K.

1. *Briefwechsel.*
2. Franklin Delano Roosevelt had died April 12, 1945.

Mann to Kahler

Pacific Palisades
May 1, 1945[1]

Dear, good Friend:

What a pleasure your letter was! And we certainly shouldn't be casting stones about silence. We are in our own glass house as far as that goes, and can also only offer by way of apology the well-known botherations, the affairs and trifles, the cares, the routine, the demands of the times. What you write about present developments — all long anticipated, coming too late, and yet staggering as reality — we have read with unanimous applause, individually and all together. You are so right when you say that the German share is only part of the general culpability of stupidity — which goes on proving itself invincible. But I must again insist that the Germans have played a special, terribly authentic role in the drama. Someone with so profound a knowedge of the German character in history would be the last to deny that.[2] How inadequately little I will be able to say about that shortly, in the lecture that you may be hearing! I have tried to find the middle course between apologia and denial, and intend to declare frankly "that I also have it all inside myself." We must not go around describing ourselves as the "good" Germany, in contrast to the "wicked" Germany with which we supposedly had nothing to do. The "wicked" is the "good" Germany whose goodness turned to wickedness.

You are right; what is the point of a long letter when we shall be seeing each other soon. Erika is with us, and on the 24th we shall be going by way of Chicago to Washington, where I am to speak at the Library on the 29th. On June 3d or 4th we will in all likelihood turn up in the Bedford [Hotel] in New York, and on the 8th I repeat the lecture at Hunter College. But on June 6th we shall be at Bruno Walter's in the evening — he and Bronislav Hubermann[3] are going to play for us. You must come to that!

Whatever possesses you — reading the manuscript? I must say I was truly alarmed to hear it. The book is a secret, you know, and for the present a completely private experiment — as yet I can't imagine publishing it. I don't regard Lowe-Porter as a reader; she is a mute instrument, never lets out a peep. And here you are, simply going ahead and reading it. Please don't pass it on to anyone!

Roosevelt — let me not speak of it. This is no longer the country to which we came. One feels orphaned and abandoned. But I suppose it was just as well this way for him.

What a *porcheria* again, this ringing speech of *Dönitz*[4] to nation and army on the Führer's heroic death. *P.M.*[5] queried me by telegram today: "Do you believe that Hitler is dead?" I replied: "Who cares?"

Give my regards to Broch and all the heroes. See you soon.

Yours,

Thomas Mann

1. *Letters.*

2. An allusion to Kahler's book *Der Deutsche Charakter in der Geschichte Europas* (1937).

3. Bronislav Hubermann (1882-1947), the celebrated violinist.

4. Karl Dönitz (b. 1891), Hitler's Grand Admiral, who formed a new government after Hitler's death.

5. New York newspaper, now defunct.

Mann to Kahler

Pacific Palisades

October 7, 1945[1]

Dear Kahler:

Your sixtieth is impending; it's the fourteenth of this month; you cannot deceive me, so let me congratulate you very heartily, dear friend, and thank you for all the good and fine things you have given us and for your many years of constancy, your intelligent sympathy with my own trying and laborious work. I must also congratulate you, and with sincere respect, for the way you have withstood the crass vicissitudes of life, have adapted to entirely changed conditions, to a foreign land, to a different language, and through it all have held your own in a manly and engaging fashion. That is admirable, impressive and moving; I cannot forbear to say it. The rest, or a little of the rest, is set down in the little congratulatory article,[2] the manuscript and copy of which I am enclosing as a modest birthday gift. I wrote it for the stouthearted *Deutsche Blätter* of Santiago de Chile, which is unfortunately about to fold unless someone helps it, and who is likely to help it? They sent me an S.O.S. letter saying they could not continue without a subsidy of about 5000 dollars. Their Dr. Kaskel[3] here has tried everything imaginable, including the Carl Schurz Society, but in vain, and now they are writing *me* that they prefer "not to take the important decision and not act too hastily without giving you the opportunity to intervene with advice and action." But for heaven's sake, what am I to do? When I think of all that I did, how I humiliated myself, how many rebuffs I received in the effort to save Klaus's *Decision*,[4] which really deserved to survive and to which he was devoted! No use. So I shall only be able to say to Rukser and Theile: "Even Patroclus died."[5] Or have you any ideas of what could be done in Princeton? Here nobody even knows what a magazine is, let alone takes any interest in a German magazine. The Jews too don't want to hear about it. *Il n'y a qu'eux,* and the *Deutsche Blätter* is thoroughly Aryan. Nevertheless I intend to speak to the people in the Jewish Club and the Pacific Press.

Number 28, in which you are to be celebrated, has at any rate gone into print. But it is so far away! Don't you think my little article ought to be published here somewhere, too? In *Aufbau* again? How boring — always the same paper! Maybe in the *Staatszeitung?* Because politically the *Volkszeitung*[6] is getting to be too *meschugge* [crazy] for me.

We had the grandchildren from San Francisco with us for

four weeks, a relief to the young parents and naturally a burden to us, but also a great deal of amusement and delight. The five-year-old, Frido, especially, is a regular prince of the elves in appearance, graceful, charming, ingratiating, and with a touch of mischief, in short very attractive and slightly worrisome in regard to the future. He was long ago assigned a part in the *Faustus,*[7] toward the end, which I occasionally try to envision, but *une mer à boire* still lies before it. Lowe-Porter will shortly receive a pile of new manuscript.

Now we are again utterly alone with the poodle. Our friends are dying away: Frank,[8] who was pleasant, and then the more richly gifted Werfel. Even their widows are going to the East. The Neumanns[9] and Leonhard Frank are not what *you* would be if you were here — may things work out so that some day you are!

So both of us wish you a glorious birthday with your dear mother and estimable friends who esteem you. I am counting on a bright Indian summer Sunday for you. That, after all, is a reasonable certainty in your climate. Here, for an entire week until day before yesterday, we had a fantastic burning heat, both enervating and stimulating. It made sleeping difficult. Then, without any crisis, hard to say why, it yielded to cooler winds. This weather is totally fickle and unpredictable. There are too many components — desert, ocean, mountain — all affecting one another, and so the forecasts are more frequently wrong than "back home in Dachau."

Yours,

Thomas Mann

1. *Briefwechsel.*

2. Thomas Mann, "Erich von Kahler: Zum sechzigsten Geburtstag," *Deutsche Blätter,* 3, No. 28 (1945); in *Altes und Neues.*

3. Josef Kaskel, lawyer, during the war was the American agent for *Deutche Blätter* in the United States.

4. Klaus Mann's magazine *Decision: A Review of Free Culture*

was published in New York from January 1941 to January–February 1942.

5. Udo Rukser (b. 1892) and Albert Theile (b. 1904) were the editors of the *Deutsche Blätter,* which was published from January 1943 to November–December 1946. Patroclus, in Homer's *Iliad,* is the friend of Achilles who, fighting in Achilles' armor, is slain by Hector.

6. *Aufbau* (New York), *Staatszeitung und Herold* (New York), *Volkszeitung* (New York).

7. See Mann to Kahler, December 31, 1941, note 8.

8. Bruno Frank.

9. Alfred Neumann (1895-1952), writer, emigrated to Italy and southern France in 1933, to the United States in 1940.

Mann to Kahler

Pacific Palisades
October 11, 1945[1]

Dear friend Kahler:

A small birthday packet was dispatched a few days ago. But I want to add these lines right away, to ask you what you think about the case of the *Deutsche Blätter,* because until you have had a chance to comment I would rather not say anything to Herr Kaskel and the good people in Santiago. For it appears that my own comment, if it turns out to be negative, would be decisive for the magazine's ceasing publication.

It is beyond question, of course, that the *Deutsche Blätter,* this truly well-meaning and well-made magazine, should go on. But there is much to be said for the argument that these exile magazines have now fulfilled their mission and that if they want to survive they would do better to move to Germany, there to work for moral reconstruction on the spot. Chiefly, though, on purely practical grounds it seems doubtful that the needed 5000 dollars for the *Deutsche Blätter* can be

[103]

raised. Consequently, I can scarcely advise making the attempt.

Let me, then, repeat my question, whether you see any way to save the magazine and whether you think that an action supported by us has the slightest prospect of success. I would be grateful to have word from you soon, so that I can give Messrs. Ruckser and Theile my final opinion, possibly transmitting it through Dr. Kaskel.

Cordially yours,
Thomas Mann

1. Princeton.

Kahler to Mann

Princeton
October 14, 1945[1]

My dear Friend:

I preferred not to know that I am sixty, and should like to forget it again as quickly as possible. This day seems to have come upon me overnight; but it could not have been brought to my awareness in any gentler, more comforting fashion than by the truly touching tributes my friends and others close to me have been offering. And most especially the wonderful, overwhelmingly good and honored words you have bestowed on me, publicly and privately, have cast a golden glow upon this otherwise rather dreary day. My deepest and sincerest thanks for that — although all this, it seems to me, lies beyond anything that one can express thanks for, and therefore puts all thanks to shame. I take you at your words and receive it all as a pledge of your friendship, which is one of the most precious good things in my life.

Since the matter is pressing, I'll answer your question about the *Deutsche Blätter* promptly. It would be sad to see this magazine fold, and I think we ought to do all we can to keep it going. Its intellectual level has fluctuated, I grant — although it has more and more improved and consolidated its gains recently. And on the whole it has never completely lost its somewhat improvised character; that has been due to the difficult circumstances and the place of publication. But it possesses something far more valuable, a fine, courageous, and — something rare in general nowadays and especially among Germans — sure-footed moral attitude, equally distant from turncoatism and desertion from German destiny, and from unthinking indignation at what is being done to the Germans today, such as we often encounter nowadays among honest, completely creditable, thoroughly anti-Nazi Germans. It is true, a great deal is being done to the Germans today. The irresponsibility and vapidity of the so-called liberators surpass all expectations. But we cannot and must not protest against it without being constantly aware of what the Germans have done themselves. *A qui le dis-je!*

The *Deutsche Blätter* has held to the right mean between these two extremes in an exemplary fashion. And therefore I think that it is needed today more than ever, is in fact irreplaceable. The *Neue Rundschau,* once it is renovated and freshened up and resumes its old tradition,[2] has other tasks. And even if it takes the same ideological direction, which it ought to do, it will be burdened as it is by that very tradition and by the imprint of S. Fischer or Bermann Fischer. It will not be able to exert the same moral effect as — that is the way things are and will remain for a considerable time to come — so pronouncedly "Aryan" an enterprise as the *Deutsche Blätter.* The proper attitude must come from the "Aryan" side, and wield its influence.

I would not even think it advisable for such a magazine to move to Germany at the present moment — although, as I understand it, such a step is not even under discussion, but only cessation or continuance. For it is highly doubtful whether it would be able to maintain the proper independent posture there. Rather, I fear that it would soon fall under the influence of the Occupation authorities or of this or that political party. In any case it would be caught up in the tangle of unavoidable terrible conflicts that must be expected. Magazines will certainly be springing up in Germany soon, whenever the technical conditions permit, but they will scarcely fulfill the mission that the *Deutsche Blätter* has had. In the next few years only Germans abroad will be able to maintain an independent attitude and preserve an unclouded vision. And I could well imagine that such a periodical might exert from outside a certain influence upon German developments, upon the development of world Germanism and of a cosmopolitan Germany. That could be accompanied by the growing participation of forces within the country. That very process, a reciprocal influencing from within and without upon an excessively parochial, excessively nationalistic German base, might greatly promote a gradual spiritual purgation and inner transformation.

Where the money is to come from is, of course, another question. I thought of the Oberlander Foundation in Philadelphia, or else concerned and broad-minded and well-heeled German-Americans. We would have to make them understand the meaning and mission of such a magazine in the manner I have suggested above, and impress the urgency of the need upon them. I should think such people must exist, but I really don't have any overview of such circles. Provided with your desire, your authority, and a few explanatory words from you, Dr. Kaskel might try once more. (Niebuhr[3] might also be enlisted for the purpose.) This time, in the face of the frightful Jewish misery, support can scarcely be expected from the Jews; and for the reasons I suggested I would not even think it desirable to obtain the backing of Jewish money. It would then be so easy to discredit the magazine on that basis.

As for your kindly eulogy of me, I would of course gladly bask in its radiance in this country too, but preferably not in the *Staatszeitung,* which still strikes me as rather fishy. Nor, you are right, in the *Volkszeitung.* So all that remains is the stale, dreary *Aufbau* once again — which I leave up to your judgment. But it would be more important, i.e., more useful for my books, if your words, with a few slight modifications, that is, shifts of accent from the German to the American audience, could appear somewhere in English. The *Saturday Review of Lit.* would probably be glad to publish them. But that is only a timid suggestion — I truly do not want you to go to additional trouble over this.

I am hungrily awaiting the continuation of the *Faust,* which I hope will soon reach Lowe-Porter. You do not say how it is going.

We are delighted that the Borgeses will be in the vicinity for a while. Next Friday I shall be seeing them for the first time at a small party that the Kurt Wolffs are arranging for me.

Golo has at last written me a letter that gladdened me, in spite of its thoroughly depressed tone. His book, thank God, is at last being printed. Where are Erika and Klaus? When will the speech on Germany be published in Washington? Questions and more questions — what a pity we are so far apart. At least it is good that you have resisted the calls from Germany! I was a little alarmed. Here, too, there are many changes. The good Sessionses,[4] whom I am so fond of, are gone; he has received a much better appointment at Berkeley. The Lowes are going to England. On the other hand, happily, the Shenstones[5] have come back.

Your magical wish actually presented me with an Indian Summer day to inaugurate my own Indian Summer. It looks benevolently in through my window. Please tell **Katia** many thanks and all the best. I shall be writing her soon. — In grateful attachment,

Ever yours,
E. K.

Belated thanks also for your fine talk at the *Nation* dinner.[6] I am happy to have it.

1. *Briefwechsel.*

2. The *Neue Rundschau,* Germany's leading literary magazine before the Nazi era, which had ceased publication after the issue of January 1944, began publication again in June 1945.

3. Reinhold Niebuhr (1892-1971), American theologian and social philosopher, the author of many books.

4. Roger Sessions (b. 1896), composer, professor of music at Princeton and subsequently at Berkeley.

5. Allen Shenstone (b. 1893, Toronto) was then professor of physics.

6. Address delivered June 25, 1945, at the testimonial dinner of the *Nation* Associates in honor of Thomas Mann at the Waldorf-Astoria Hotel; in *Addresses in Honor of Dr. Thomas Mann* (New York, 1945).

Mann to Kahler

Pacif. Palisades
December 29, 1945[1]

Dear Friend:

Here are the two letters from Pree.[2] They are much the most sensible things that have come to me out of Germany.

Please thank Broch from me for his letter. He is of course right: Fascism is not downed, is not beaten; there is no intention of defeating it. Instead it is engaged in steady growth, in Europe, here, everywhere. The change of mood to pro-German and hence antiexile is highly interesting. My letter to Molo,[3] for all the good it did here, is extremely unpopular over there, and not only in Germany. Even Schlumberger in Paris has written a nasty article[4] about it. At best, those who are kindly disposed toward me *excuse* it — as they also do my radio broadcasts during the war,[5] declaring that they are already worthless and testify only to political ignorance. It is all very curious.

What a good period the war was! Deceptively good — Broch is quite right.

Cross the threshold of the year bravely and in good spirits. At Christmas I called attention to *Man the Measure* in a Chicago newspaper. But of course they don't send a clipping.

Warm regards,
T. M.

1. *Briefwechsel.*

2. Emil Preetorius. See Kahler to Mann, January 22, 1946.

3. September 7, 1945 (in *Letters,* p. 478): "Warum ich nicht nach Deutschland zurückgehe" ("Why I Do Not Return to Germany"), *Aufbau* (New York), 2 (September 28, 1945). Walter von Molo (1880-1958), a novelist who was president of the Prussian Writers' Academy, 1928-1930, was a favorite of the Nazi regime because of his nationalistic emotionalism and was for a time a champion of Hitlerism but later retired to his estate. He remained a member of the Academy, however, and continued to write unmolested.

4. Jean Schlumberger, "Pourquoi je n'entre pas en Allemagne ("Why I Do Not Enter Germany"): Lettre de Thomas Mann à Walter von Molo: Extraits et commentaires," *Terre des hommes,* November 10, 1946. Schlumberger (1877-1968), French novelist, was associated with André Gide on the *Nouvelle Revue Française.*

5. *Deutsche Hörer! Fünfundfünfzig Radiosendungen nach Deutschland* (2d, enlarged ed.; Stockholm, 1945).

Mann to Kahler

Dear Kahler:

Greetings. And please do send Pree's letter back. I still owe an answer to the second and need the military address.

What has been happening to Mrs. Lowe? She was going to send the manuscript of the novel, all there is of it so far, back to me once more before she left for England. I have a long list of corrections I want to make. Has her departure been postponed? Or has the manuscript by mistake gone along to England? Third possibility: Do you have it? In that case, please send it right away, well packed! I've written to Lowe-Porter, but on thinking it over it seems best that I send the letter to you, so that you can either give it to her if she is still there or forward it to her London address, which you will know.

Many thanks, and all the best from house to house!

Yours,
Thomas Mann

1. Princeton.

Kahler to Mann

My dear Friend:

I have long been wanting to write to you again, but a great deal of urgent work while I was droopy from grippe has only added to my normal negligence about letters. In any case

I have myself turned into a convoluted sentence, and am growing more and more impatient and enervated as a result — in imitation of and sympathy with you. In the autumn I set to work on the democracy book[2] (which in itself was a side issue) and thought I would be sticking to it no matter what. But all sorts of small matters that could not be put off intervened: the obituary for Beer-Hofmann,[3] a duty from the heart; an essay on "the ethical and psychological consequences of the 'Atomic Age' " for the *American Scholar*,[4] suggested by the good Dean Gauss,[5] whom I did not want to disappoint; Bermann's proposal that he do a volume of my essays,[6] which has meant considerable assembling and revising, especially since I would like to include a very important preliminary study for my book on the foundations and premises of our present-day knowledge and therefore must think everything through once more from A to Z. Not to mention Oprecht's and Kurt Wolff's insistence on the German version of *Man the Measure*. Enough and more than enough for someone as slow-paced as I am. In March I am to give a ten-day seminar at Black Mountain College in North Carolina; this has already been postponed three times. And yet I have resisted with an iron will all sorts of trifles that have come my way. What must you endure if even I, who after all enjoy relative anonymity in this country, am so pressed.

Mrs. Lowe, who has just spent a few days as our guest, since she no longer has a home here, has by now surely written you about the manuscript. She still has need of it before leaving for England, and will send it back to you before her departure. Meanwhile, I have devoured the new sections up to the magnificent painting of the cosmos.[7] My admiration and enthusiasm grow and grow. It is a masterpiece, with its successively overflowing, ebullient, ever bolder breakthroughs opening out into ever richer prospects, yet with the full texture of allusions. It is growing more and more complex; and I tremble with awe at what you may still have before you in the way of dramatic intensification and symphonic handling of the motifs. What control with such richness! At the same time the reader feels your own tenseness here as in scarcely any other of your books; and this passionate participation is also to the good. There is so much to be said about specifics that I must renounce any attempt to do it in a letter. Let us forbear until the book is available in print and I have mastered the whole of it in tranquillity. I took a special and personal pleasure in the wonders of the ocean depths, for ever since my youth I have been fascinated by those promorphic and metamorphic creatures of the underworld, which are still well-nigh as flexible as at Creation. It is also amusing to meet Annette and Reisiger[8] being so quietly themselves in the midst of this volcanically heaving cosmopsychic life process.

I can imagine how you must be bothered by anything that distracts you from the pursuit of this plan. Once begun, an intellectual fabric of such complexity hangs in the air — everything depends on carrying it through right to the end without tangling it and without losing a single thread. What a burden on the mind such a delicately ethereal thing can be is something that can only be appreciated by one who has once become involved in — *ceteris imparibus* [everything else being unequal] — something similar. Yet the obligations and responsibilities continue, and it is necessary to think decisions through precisely, down to the very language used. German matters in particular — how hard it is, how hard to see and to pursue the proper mean between all the extremes and simplifications! I have the fiercest discussions with one side and with the other — with Einstein, say, whose hostility toward everything German is boundless, and along with him a large number of well-intentioned and intelligent persons who simply react to this problem with instant blind fury;

and on the other side, *with the Germans who once more, in their bitterness over the obvious sins of the Allies, have forgotten what endless harm has emanated from their own people.*[9] That is the problem of the Chicago appeal.[10] We signed it, and for my part I am glad I did sign it; it was an emotional relief, a moral alibi. For what the Allies have done and are doing there — *burning and letting rot army provisions and clothing when all around them people are starving and freezing, blowing up factories when the people have no roofs over their heads, the cruelty of the Czech and Polish mass expulsions on the verge of winter, the whole brutal indifference and businesslike efficiency with which the future of Europe is once again being forfeited* — we cannot be silent about all that without becoming accessories to it. But I grant that the appeal is feeble and one-sided, and leaves a great deal unsaid that should have been said for the sake of balance and to distinguish it from other highly suspect German-American actions. It should have spoken of *the laxity of the proceedings against the Nazis and the conspiracy of silence (even in Germany) about the German resistance movements, which were much more extensive than people here know, of the open favoring and employment of Nazis, especially in the French zone — sins, sins that will bear their dreadful fruits. Is this what has come of the years of blather about "re-education"? Is this what has come of the Office of Psychological Warfare and the humbug about sociopsychological research that the whole country is full of?* We receive regular reports from friends who are now holding official posts in Germany. *While everybody is enjoying the Nuremberg show trials against the top people, who were done for long ago, a host of little Nazis (block wardens, minor officials, etc.) have been quietly taking over and are already crushing the honestly antifascist people under the eyes and the patronage of the military government.* What will happen once *the occupation armies are disbanded,*

[113]

*as of course they will be all too soon under the emotional pres-
sure from those uninstructed "boys," who want nothing but
to go home?* And the exponents of realpolitik, the Vansittarts,
Schwarzschilds,[11] and so on, who have demanded a fifty-year
occupation of Germany! *But in the face of such rapid forget-
fulness and indifference on the part of the Allies, in the face
of the examples they present, in the face of such confirmation
of all the Nazi predictions, how can one expect, let alone demand, of the average German that he show prompt repentance
and a sincere change of heart? Such an awakening from ten
years of stupor and isolation, such a process of recollection
and conversion, takes time and psychic energy, and surround-
ings that promote decency and demote baseness. Under present
conditions, the only kind of person who can afford such a
change of heart is one who desires and needs goodness for its
own sake, without considering the consequences and the values
he sees ascendant all around him.* And how many such persons
are there in the whole wide world, let alone in Europe after a
decade of terror?

And that also brings us to the problem of Pree. I am
simultaneously sending the letters back to you by ordinary
mail, and here in advance is the military address: Lt. Gerard
W. Speyer 0-2026480, Information Control Div., Publishing
Operations Section, USFET, APO 757 c/o Postmaster N.Y.,
N.Y. The letters excited me enormously. They evoked him
completely for me, his general weakness and his personal,
quite feminine devotedness — I would be tempted to say
loyalty, if that word did not have its intellectual aspects as well;
how can anyone be wholly loyal to a friend if he allies himself
with elements that would destroy the friend's very being? How
furious I was with him when, in letters to a mutual friend,
he spoke to her of the Führer without quotation marks, boasting
that in Bayreuth Hitler acted as his patron and supporter.
How furious I was when he published essays in the *Völkischer*

Beobachter.[12] And yet the fury has subsided; I can no longer summon it up. And when I now read these pitiable letters, so full of a craving to resume relations, to know what has been going on, I am weaponless. I know so very well how he feels. So please give him my regards when you write to him. Can we assume that he has enough to eat, being in Bavaria?

The *Deutsche Blätter* people have informed me of your objections. May I once again put in a word for them? I don't think one can ask them to accept the Potsdam decisions[13] as just and correct once and for all. They aren't so at all, even though for the moment everyone will have to bow to them. The December issue has just arrived — thanks again!

And now that is all for today — this letter is far too long, although it contains only a few of the many things I urgently wanted to say to you. They will have to be postponed.

I am avidly waiting for the continuation of Adrian's[14] career, and also for the Nietzsche speech[15] on which you are working, as Kurt Wolff has told me.

Fond regards to Katia, who will certainly be hearing from me shortly, and all good wishes to you yourself.

Yours,
E. K.

Broch sends his warm regards. He has written an excellent memorandum[16] for the Chicago people, setting forth the needed revisions on the appeal. Unfortunately, it will probably arrive too late.

1. *Briefwechsel.*

2. "Das Schicksal der Demokratie" ("The Fate of Democracy"), lecture, 1945, delivered to the *Kreis der deutschen Blätter,* New York; in expanded form in *Synopsis: Festgabe für Alfred Weber,* ed. Edgar Salin (Heidelberg, 1948).

3. The obituary for Richard Beer-Hofmann was published in January 1946 in the *Neue Rundschau* and in April 1946 in *Commentary.*

4. "The Reality of Utopia," *American Scholar,* 15, No. 2 (1946). See the next letter, note 2.

5. Christian Gauss (1878-1951), professor of French literature and writer, was at this time dean at Princeton University.

6. The volume of essays, *Die Verantwortung des Geistes: Gesammelte Aufsätze* ("The Responsibility of Mind: Collected Essays"), was not published until 1952, in Frankfurt.

7. Chapter xxvii of *Doctor Faustus*. At this time Thomas Mann was already working on the *Apocalipsis cum figuris*, chapter xxxiv.

8. The writer Annette Kolb (1875-1967) appears in *Doctor Faustus* as Jeanette Scheurl. The writer and translator Hans Reisiger (1884-1966) was the model for Rüdiger Schildknapp.

9. The passages printed in italics were either underlined in red pencil or marked in the margin by Thomas Mann.

10. An appeal sponsored by James Franck of Chicago to collect money for the starving Germans. James Franck (1882-1961), the physicist, received the Nobel Prize in 1925. In 1935 he emigrated to the United States, where he taught at Johns Hopkins and the University of Chicago.

11. Lord Robert Vansittart (1881-1957) was the British diplomat whose anti-German stance became a byword (Vansittartism). Leopold Schwarzschild (1891-1950), publicist, in the early thirties was the editor of the Berlin weekly *Das Tagebuch,* which he continued in Paris exile as *Das neue Tagebuch.*

12. The organ of the German Nazi party.

13. The Potsdam Conference, July 17–August 2, 1945, decreed the extirpation of Nazism, the abolition of Nazi organizations and laws, the disbandment of the German armed forces, the trial of war criminals, the democratization and decentralization of the German government, and control of education in Germany by the Allies.

14. Adrian Leverkühn, the protagonist of *Doctor Faustus.*

15. "Nietzsche's Philosophy in the Light of Recent History," a lecture delivered at the meeting of the PEN Club in Zurich on June 2, 1947; in *Last Essays,* trans. Richard and Clara Winston (New York, 1959).

16. A copy of the fifteen-page memorandum ("Notes to an Appeal in Behalf of the German People") was enclosed with a letter from Hermann Broch of January 30, 1946, to Professor James Franck of Chicago. On January 31, 1946, Broch sent copies of this letter and of the memorandum to Thomas Mann. The documents are preserved in the Thomas Mann Archives in Zurich.

Mann to Kahler

Pacific Palisades
February 5, 1946[1]

Dear friend Kahler:

Your good long letter of January 22 is in my hands, and with it the fine essay on the reality of utopia,[2] which will be an ornament of the *American Scholar* and the *Neue Rundschau*. I was deeply moved as I read it. It has that wise and heart-warming tone I have already found so stirring in your recent work. There is nobody else who could characterize the vital either-or that confronts our civilization better and more affectingly.

On top of all that you have found the time and energy, while sending the Pree letters back to me, to write so copiously to me — an act of true friendship. Naturally, your encouraging remarks about the novel moved me most of all and did me the most good. How badly one needs such comforting! How badly, in the struggle with such a devilish work, one needs a good word of encouragement. But far more important, of course, are all your painfully correct comments on the situation in Germany, all that you say about the mishandling of the world's affairs in general. And this in turn brings me to our friend Broch's impressive note to James Franck. Many thanks to him for sending it to me. I read it with approval and a heavy heart, wondering whether Broch realized that with his only too trenchant objections and corrections he was really invalidating the appeal issued by that kind and good man James Franck. It would hardly be possible to revise the appeal in line with Broch's proposals, especially since these do not belong in an appeal at all, but at best in a petition to the State Department or the Military Government in Germany. Nor can I say I am in full agreement with every one of his suggestions and formulations. But I agree entirely with the negative aspects, that is, with his criticisms of the appeal. What he says fully clarified and corroborated for me the serious doubts I had about signing. At the time, in a letter to Borgese, who sent me the appeal, I indicated my reservations in no uncertain terms, although I did not go into detail. And in fact I signed only because, if there were to be any such action, the absence of my name would seem too ostentatious and nasty. I agree that this action can all too easily be identified with tendencies and machinations that are foreign and hostile to us; this is a serious danger, and the experiences I have recently had, in America and Germany both, in connection with a similar campaign, an appeal for feeding German children, are so discouraging that I truly shrink from any repetition. But now, since Broch's note has more or less reopened the discussion of the matter, I have been unable to refrain from writing a letter to Franck, in which I gently and with many declarations of sympathy for the nobility of his intentions, urge him to drop a matter which will certainly do no good but which will produce a host of annoyances for us.

It is a sad pity that we are so far apart. How good it would be to be able to discuss all these things thoroughly with each other. I am excited, half depressed and half pricked by curiosity, at the renewed prospect of a trip to Europe, on the basis of invitations coming from there. That plan, already deferred to a distant future, has once again come to the fore and is moving closer. I am supposed to give lectures in Sweden, England, France, Belgium, Holland, and Switzerland: and in the course of such a trip, naturally, a visit to Germany cannot be left out. If I ever want to turn up there again, I shall have to do so soon; otherwise it will no longer be possible to span the gulf. Nothing has been decided as yet, but negotiations are in progress.

Warm regards! Whether or not Europe is our destination

in May, in any case we will be coming to the East. The secretary[3] also sends her warm regards.

Yours,
Thomas Mann

1. Princeton.

2. "Die Wirklichkeit der Utopie," *Neue Rundschau*, 3 (1946) ("The Reality of Utopia," *American Scholar,* 15, No. 2 [1946]).

3. I.e., Katia Mann.

Mann to Kahler

Pacific Palisades
February 13, 1946[1]

Dear Kahler:

Just a hasty word of thanks for your letter. You are right in every word you say. Insistent warnings to stay away have been coming to me from all sides. Anyhow, the project can scarcely be carried out, quite aside from the German problem. Nowhere do they have so much as warm water for washing, and the prices are such that a stay of a few months would, I think, consume all our savings.

I am glad that your study of German responsibility will reach Germany. It is very well balanced and at any rate puts off until the end the things the Germans *don't* want to hear. They are frightful people — don't take it amiss that I say this! If my forbearing letter of apology,[2] the whole second half of which was sheer love, so embittered them that I can no longer show myself there, there is nothing to be done and they cannot be helped. It is simply that the letter rests on the assumption of a common hatred for Nazism, and that this assumption was *wrong*. It is the old Nazi country and will remain so. The only hope is to keep it powerless for a hundred years.

[119]

Golo writes that Wiechert's[3] virtue has rather gone to his head and that he has occasionally referred to himself as the "father of truth." Now I hear that he has illegally distributed a pamphlet mocking the American occupation troops. It is called "The Rich Man and Poor Lazarus" and is full of poetic self-pity. Incidentally, he recommends patience, not for a year not for twelve, but for 1200! I've said, I would be content with 100.

Franck's appeal is going out. I did not, of course, withdraw my signature.[4] How could I have! But I would have preferred to join in signing *your* message.[5]

Don't imagine that I shall be making friends of the Germans when *Faustus* is published there. They're not to be won over so easily.

Yours,
T. M.

1. Princeton. Kahler's letter to which this replies is missing.

2. Mann's letter to Walter von Molo of September 7, 1945. See Mann to Kahler, December 29, 1945.

3. Ernst Wiechert (1887-1950), writer, who was sentenced to several months in a concentration camp for his circular letters and speeches opposing the Nazis, emigrated to Switzerland in 1948 and died there.

4. See Kahler to Mann, January 22, 1946; and Mann to Kahler, February 5, 1946. Einstein refused to sign and tried to persuade Kahler and Broch to withdraw their signatures.

5. Mann is referring to "The Responsibility of Mind," Kahler's essay in honor of Mann's seventieth birthday. See Kahler's *The Orbit of Thomas Mann* (Princeton, N.J., 1969).

Kahler to Mann

My dear Friend:

Unfortunately, I cannot come to you in person, to bring you my happiness and my good wishes, and to chat with you at length and leisurely, as I should so like to do, and as would be appropriate to this stage of your convalescence — more so than in April, when the forthcoming operations[2] dominated everyone's mood. But there are conferences here, and time and money are short. So I must come to you again on wretched paper. I had so enjoyed imagining how I would be able to participate for a few days in the revival of your health and vigor, a process we always watch with pleasure, as we do the growth of a child. There is a certain similarity, for it is truly a new person that emerges from an illness, as I know from my own experience and as you, a newcomer to this phase of life, will now discover. One encounters the world all over again as if for the first time, and one's first reaction to it has the same irritability and sensitivity as that of small children, until these reactions are replaced by astonishment, cognition, but also by new perceptions. It is lovely, particularly lovely; for we never live so close to objects, so sensuously close and at the same time so knowledgeably close, as we do in such moments. Everything is very slow and careful, as if I lived in slow motion; and we are given time and peace to experience it. Later on we will no longer have that.

But why am I needlessly telling you all this? In the first place, you are experiencing it yourself; and in the second place, you long ago prelived it, in keeping with your profession. For my part, I have projected myself into it and savored it just because I have been denied the pleasure of being with you during these days.

As for myself, I have been compelled to deal much too much with the world at large, which is more abominable than ever. If I were in your place, I would use the opportunity to take a brief vacation from it, practice escapism, look away, and instead of reading newspapers turn to something good, old, dusty, the dustier and more idyllically remote the better. I wish I had the right to be just a wee bit idyllic, to tell myself a story altogther distant from world constitutions, articles on the atom bomb, books on democracy and sociology, committees (I am on several, alas), and so on. How I long for that — but for heaven's sake, this is just between the two of us; don't tell the sultry secretary-general,[3] for she'll think me a defeatist again; and hide this letter in your deepest drawer. Incidentally, of course, it wouldn't work. Before you know it, that story would veer back to the world's confusions, which we have in ourselves, carry with us at every moment, everywhere we go. (A propos, do you have No. 29 of the *Deutsche Blätter?* There is an essay[4] — or rather lecture — of mine in it that I would like to have you read. If not, I'll send it to you.)

If you have a euphoric minute, such as often comes as one is convalescing, please let me have a few penciled lines. That would be a delight!

Get better and better, give my regards to the family circle, and know that you are the recipient of my heartfelt wishes and are constantly accompanied in thought by

Forever yours,
E. K.

The whole house sends you good wishes and greetings. And people are constantly asking us how you are. I cannot possibly write down all their names; it's a telephone book.

Karl Wolfskehl, from whom I have just had a letter, sends you regards and his "cordial respects."

1. *Briefwechsel.*
2. In April 1946, Thomas Mann had undergone a lung operation

in Chicago. He has related the course of it in *The Story of a Novel:*
The Genesis of "Doctor Faustus" (New York, 1961).

3. Katia Mann.

4. "Das Problem der Demokratie," *Deutsche Blätter*, 4, No. 29
(1946).

Mann to Kahler

Billings Memorial Hospital
Chicago
May 15, 1946[1]

Dear friend Kahler:

Many thanks for your delightful, entertaining visit by letter.
I am in no condition to return so much goodness with anything good, for my life at present is as impoverished in
thoughts as in deeds; it's really a case of rather too little of
anything. And yet I may say that I went through this whole
unexpected adventure with serious attentiveness, although
without any thoughts worth communicating, and can be content with myself insofar as the thing may be thought of as an
opportunity to show fortitude. I can even pride myself on
having accomplished a few "deeds," in the active sense of the
word, for in this situation I displayed an almost uncanny
psychological preference for passive accomplishments. I went
in for being a model patient, a role which after all has its
dubious aspects. And yet I have enjoyed seeing how my good-
natured and patient constitution helped the helpers to accomplish something very nearly sensational in the way of a smooth
and successful operation entirely without complications. "The
most *elegant* operation in many years," the doctors said. At
the same time the business was no joke, as the tremendous
scar running from my chest to my back distinctly shows. Without codeine I still would not be able to take the pain of the
healing process. But I am walking effortlessly, was outside in

the wheelchair yesterday, and must only avoid moving too rapidly, since I still tend to be short of breath, and probably will for months to come.

I cannot praise the hospital enough; Adams[2] proved to be first-class, and the preliminary and postoperational treatment was perfect; every factor was taken into consideration. I have gone through the whole gamut: bronchoscopy, blood transfusions, pneumothorax, etc.; but everything was done in the most considerate, most progressive manner.

We mean to set out on the 24th and hope to drive into our flower-filled garden on Sunday the 26th, with Erika. I must put my mind entirely to finishing the novel. It deserves that on the whole, although some things may have gone wrong in the details. Toward the end I was writing it against the counterpressure of the illness. But in a work that deserves the name, not everything has to be successful. I am reading — for the first time as a whole, I think — *Der grüne Heinrich*.[3] It has its weaknesses, prolixities, vexations, but is truly a *work* after my own heart.

Isn't the last issue of the *Rundschau* excellent? Not least because of your splendid essay.[4] A quotation from Nietzsche, incidentally: "I am speaking about democracy as of something *to come.*"

Thanks once more for your visit. I hope we shall see one another soon. Give Broch my best regards and remember me to your dear mother.

Yours,
T. M.

1. *Letters.*

2. William E. Adams (b. 1902), specialist in lung surgery at Billings Memorial Hospital in Chicago. Dr. Adams saved Mann's life.

3. *Der grüne Heinrich* (1854-1855; *Green Henry,* 1960) is an autobiographical novel by the Swiss novelist Gottfried Keller (1819-1890).

4. "Die Wirklichkeit der Utopie."

Mann to Kahler

Dear Erich:

Is it possible, Prince? Can an omission like this trouble your conscience? A perfectly ordinary seventy-first birthday? It's kind enough that you thought of it afterward.

I am tolerably well, and if I were more obedient and did not keep on the go as much mentally and physically, I would probably be further along by now. Still, I have gained five pounds since we have been back — *quite satisfactory*.

Having Erika here is very dear and delightful — she is writing a book about Europe. We laugh a great deal about the United States chaos — *the biggest chaos the world ever saw*.

Cordially,

Yours,
T. M.

1. *Letters.*

Kahler to Mann

Princeton
September 2, 1946[1]

My dear Friend:

It is high time for me to be writing you again. I meant to back in July, before I left for vacation, and I meant to during vacation, but the demands of the mail, especially the mail from Europe, once more swamped me. It is getting so that I ought to have a secretary, at least for current, daily matters, but I can't afford one and don't know what the end of it will be.

I was happy to hear how well you are — touch wood! — and how you are gaining weight, keeping pace with *Faust*. How much of the book still has to tucked under your belt? And is it good and weighty? I think it should be: only weightiness is good. How eager I am to see the new parts. But now that Lowe-Porter is gone, I suppose there is no prospect of my getting a look at it in the near future.

My four weeks of airing with friends in Maine and Vermont were lovely and refreshing, only slightly troubled by an injury to my foot which prevented me from swimming and walking for quite a few precious days. For the first time I saw the lovely fjords of Maine, with their intricately winding, enchanting bays and myriad baylets, where fragrant forests go right down to the coast, a wonderful combination. This is remarkable country, varied, variegated, like the many peoples that go to make up this people. The Serkins have a country house in Vermont, on the open crown of a mountain, from which you look far out over waves of wooded hills: romantic, German country, Kasper David Friedrich, Hans Thoma.[2] In the lowlands, in the vicinity of Manchester, Lake St. Catherine is Salzkammergut [Austria], and then again, a short distance away, you come into English park landscape or Scotland. But whenever I am inclined to lose myself in such associations I am always checked by that gentle, ghostly, melancholic monotony which lies like an even coating over everything and which comes from the nonhuman, from the absence of the human element, of human fertilization of the landscape, from the barrenness of a civilization insensitively and irrelevantly strewn on top of it. Even in New England, with its often charming white country houses set in the midst of their gardens, lanes, and groves, I cannot escape this feeling of the alien quality of the landscape. It *is* "colonial."

The world makes such a stench that one really wants to get farther away from it than, alas, it is possible to go. It surpasses any imaginable corrective, or even invective. Stupidity has truly assumed heroic proportions. But we too shall have to stew in the witches' cauldron they're so enthusiastically preparing for themselves. What else can we do except act as if there were still people who could be guided by what we say, as if there were still somebody who might take our words to heart?

With that in mind, I once more have two requests for you. The first concerns our good Paul Frankl[3] here, who for years has been scanting his medieval glass windows because he is obsessed by the idea of a world party of peace, peoples against governments, a "people's union" in all countries, which would force peace and cooperation upon their respective governments. Two years ago here in Princeton he founded a germinal cell of this "international,"[4] and with touching fanaticism tried to put it across. Although a few excellent persons helped him — such as Lowe, Roger Sessions, Hetty Goldman, and his own boss, the art historian Morey[5] — he is understandably having a hard time of it. Nevertheless, he has managed to set up a quite respectable group in New York, and one in Chicago. I also participated from the start, not because I hoped for much from it, but out of respect for him and his unshakable devotion to the good cause, and because I think that a good honest cause ought to be supported in any case. He now particularly wishes you to join his group, helping it by the authority of your name. I am simultaneously sending you a few pages of his program and informative material. Consider it: I don't think that by entering you would be compromising yourself in any way.

The second plea comes from *Deutsche Blätter,* and has, so I hear, already been urged by Dr. Klepper[6] in Mexico. I merely want to give it my heartfelt support. I am enclosing a letter to me from the agent of *D.B.* in Mexico, to recall the matter to your mind. I continue to think that this magazine —

more than ever today, and not least because of its effectiveness on a continent already alarmingly infected by the Nazis — is extremely necessary and worth saving.

Many thanks for your check for Pannwitz[7] and for transmitting the messages from our friend in Shanghai.[8] I have written to Mrs. O'Hara[9] and hope that you will not again be bothered by inquiries from this source.

Please write again — I do not dare to hope that we will be seeing you in the East again before too long. What a comfort that would be, and how I need it!

The very best to all of you.

Ever yours,
E. K.

Many thanks to Katia for her letter; it was a great pleasure. I'd like to write to her soon, but I don't dare make any promises.

P.S. Oh yes, via Broch and Burgmüller I am supposed to send regards from Prof. Henser (now director of the Academy of Art in Düsseldorf) and his wife (the granddaughter of Rethel).[10]

In addition, I am here copying a passage from a letter of Reisiger's to Broch dated June 23, 1946: "I have already written twice to T. M., also once to Golo M. via the Stuttgart radio. . . . But so far have no reply. Perhaps he thinks that *I* too stayed in Germany after '38 for sheer pleasure! But I really *cannot* imagine *that*. In any case I intend to write once more. I addressed the first two short letters to Princeton (in 1945). So perhaps they did not reach him at all." He writes that in May '38, after his release from arrest, he received a cable from Berkeley University (presumably at your intervention), but that the American consulate did not give him a visa because he lacked two years of teaching experience in Germany. As a result he *could not* get away. It sounds plausible.

His address, in case you have not received his letters, is Bopserstrasse 5, Stuttgart (14b). How glad he would be to know he was portrayed in your *Faust*.

1. Alice Kahler.
2. Kasper David Friedrich (1774-1840) was a German romantic landscape painter. Hans Thoma (1839-1924) was a German painter in the tradition of late German romanticism modified by the influence of Courbet.
3. Paul Frankl (1878-1962), German art critic and art historian, was a member of the Institute for Advanced Study at Princeton.
4. The People's Union for World Democracy.
5. Hetty Goldman (1881-1972), American archaeologist, was a professor in the Institute for Advanced Study at Princeton. Charles Rufus Morey (1877-1955), professor of art and archaeology at Princeton, emeritus, was cultural attaché at the U.S. Embassy, Rome, 1945-1950, acting director of the American Academy in Rome, 1945-1950, founder of the Index of Christian Art at Princeton University.
6. Unidentified.
7. Rudolf Pannwitz (1881-1969), German poet and philosopher, a disciple of Nietzsche and Stefan George, was a cofounder of the periodical *Charon*.
8. Unidentified.
9. Miss O'Hara was a long-time secretary of Agnes Meyer.
10. Herbert Burgmüller (b. 1913), writer and editor, author of *Zur Klärung der Begriffe und Neuordnung der Werte* (Munich, 1947), had been in the resistance movement against Hitler. Alfred Rethel (1816-1859) was a German historical painter.

Mann to Kahler

Pacific Palisades
September 10, 1946[1]

Dear Friend:

I was so deeply touched to receive your letter of the 2d, for I know how overburdened you are with correspondence and am therefore all the more grateful that you found the time for such a long letter. How good it would be if we were able to talk with each other again! I still have the feeling that we did not make enough use of the opportunity we had in Chicago. But perhaps it was no proper opportunity. Talking was too hard for me at the time.

Immediately after your letter came the papers concerning The People's Union for World Democracy. It goes without saying that this idea and this organization enjoy my full sympathy. The only hope of preserving peace, in the face of the stupid and criminal raving of the press and the groups that pay it, obviously lies in the natural horror of war felt by the masses, and the idea of appealing to the peoples, of summoning them and reinforcing both their good sense and their justified fear, strikes me as good and right. I am fully prepared to support that idea. Please tell your friend Paul Frankl so, and inform him that my name is at his disposal, just as yours is.

I am glad to be able to give you such a clearly affirmative answer on this point at least. For in regard to the matter of the Chilean *Deutsche Blätter,* I must fail you more and more. Dr. Klepper requested me to write to that wealthy man who is supposed to have been my schoolmate — Mr. Rudolf Groth, that is — and persuade him to hand over the $7000 that at present represents or soon will represent the magazine's deficit. Only recently Mr. Groth turned to me on behalf of his daughter, who is a student at Berkeley and would like to pay us a visit. We are glad to be helpful to her, and have already arranged about that. It is most distasteful to me to approach the man immediately with commercial requests, and I have had to tell Mr. Klepper that it would not be a matter of an investment but of a generous donation; and he adds that they do not intend to be reassured by this donation and to wait until it is used up, so that they have to go begging again, but that they mean to take steps to place the magazine on a sound financial basis. He doesn't say how they mean to do this, and the receptivity and responsiveness of the Germans in South America seem to me so slight that I have greater and greater doubts about the viability of such a magazine. I have expressed my opinion to Dr. Klepper that a well-handled liberal daily newspaper would still carry on the task that the *Deutsche Blätter* has set itself, better and with greater prospect of success. Between you and me, my skepticism is reinforced by the indubitably well-meaning but somewhat spongy and vague attitude of the magazine, which, to my feeling, much too much resembles the spirit of the "internal emigration" and, for my taste, is much too sympathetic to the ideas of the Thiesses[2] and the Wiecherts — mentalities from which I cannot expect any contribution whatsoever to the enlightenment and convalescence of Germany.

It is very good to hear that Mr. Theile will shortly be coming to the United States and will probably be passing through Los Angeles. He writes this to me and holds out the prospect of a visit. In conversation with him, perhaps, some kind of understanding can be reached.

For now, please put up with this down payment on a letter, dear friend, and warm regards from all of us. Medi is no longer here. She returned to her duties a few days ago. Erika and Klaus will probably leave us pretty much at the same time, toward the end of the month. But in compensation there is a prospect of Golo's coming; at any rate he will spend a few vacation weeks with us.

Auf Wiedersehen!

Yours,

Thomas Mann

Please let Reisiger know that no letter from him ever reached us. The Princeton address is no explanation for that, since my mail has always been forwarded from there. Incidentally,

Schildknapp[3] could have written something to his friends whenever he was abroad during the Nazi years, that is, in Holland. Yes, he did not remain in Germany for pleasure, rather because of sloth and because he was, "thank God, as it happens not a Jew" — because he thought the Nazi regime was there to stay, thought he would live better under it, and probably did live fairly well, and regarded us rather than himself and his ilk as hopeless, wrongheaded people.

I had obtained a teaching post in Berkeley for him, and guaranteed his salary. He answered the dean's cable: "Very honored, but difficulties. Letter follows." The letter never followed, and the difficulties were never defined. I have no doubt that we could have overcome them at the time, if they had lain in anything other than his sluggishness and disloyalty.

T. M.

1. Princeton.
2. Frank Thiess (b. 1890), a novelist whose work stresses robust activity, remained in Germany throughout the war.
3. See Kahler to Mann, January 22, 1946, note 8.

Mann to Kahler

Pacific Palisades
January 5, 1947[1]

Good, dear Friend:

Many thanks for your and Broch's telegram. Good Lord, yes, it does always represent a certain moral achievement to bring something of this sort to a conclusion.[2] Whether there is anything else commendable about it must be known by the One who plays such a prominent part in the book. At the moment I am totally blind to it. But we are so weak and stupid, you know: a little praise, and we are at once convinced that we have done something magnificent. "Certain patients are not hard to help," says Platen.[3]

For several days we trembled for the roof over your head, whether you could stay. The news of Einstein's generous intervention was a great relief for us too.[4]

I have my lecture in Washington on April 29.[5] Then we will come to New York and celebrate our reunion. I wonder whether this time we will continue on to London and Switzerland. *And,* inevitably, also touch upon the country of G.? *Quaeritur* [That is the question]. The trip should have been prepared long ago, but all sorts of things have intervened.

Warm regards to all of you.

Yours,
Thomas Mann

1. *Briefwechsel.*
2. *Doctor Faustus.*
3. Nicht schwer zu helfen ist gewissen Kranken:
   Ein einz'ger Wink, ein Händedruck entfaltet
   Uns Millionen liebender Gedanken.

[August von Platen, "An Schelling," *Gesammelte Werke des Grafen August von Platen* (2 vols.; Stuttgart and Tübingen, 1833), p. 97]

4. Albert Einstein lent Erich Kahler, without interest, a large sum of money for the down payment, so that Kahler was able to buy One Evelyn Place in Princeton. Mrs. Kahler reports that when Kahler asked Einstein what he would charge for the loan, Einstein replied, "Bin ich ein Shylock?"

5. "Nietzsche's Philosophy in the Light of Contemporary Events," delivered at the Library of Congress; in *Last Essays,* titled "Nietzsche's Philosophy in the Light of Recent History."

Kahler to Mann

Ithaca
December 6, 1947[1]

My dear Friend:

I am close to you, with you, frequently, and that drives me again to direct communication. First of all, when I was home in Princeton for two days at Thanksgiving, I fetched the *Faustus* which was waiting there for me — thanks, thanks to you and to fate that I may now really hold it in my hands. And I have done so with considerable emotion — in fact, was deeply stirred. For I now sense so keenly all that lies behind it, humanly, intellectually artistically, biographically, historically . . . I have been reading it — from the beginning again, of course, after first depravedly sniffing around — reading it with a full realization of all the backgrounds, as it were, yours, the German, the universal background . . . It is a true festival; all the lights have been lit. For, as it happens, I am also close to you, with you, in my class, and for the purpose of my lectures have once again traversed your whole course — from "Little Herr Friedemann" on. I filled myself in a good deal, ferreting out all sorts of hidden things I hadn't known, like the precious "Way to the Churchyard," which I enjoyed indescribably. What a way: from *Tonio Kröger* to *Faustus!*[2] How you have unfolded, out of an utterly personal core, an entire cosmos that penetrates our world in all its dimensions — the very model of an organic evolution! And how dangerous a course it was, how endangered, shot through with shuddering ambiguities, with all our dreadful problems, bloodily experienced problems. And how could it have reached its consummation except in this *Faust* of yours? But bear with me if I say no more about it today. I am to review it for the *Rundschau* — a great pleasure — and I want to approach it freshly. "Review" — see it anew — what a marvelous double meaning in this word. Well then, I shall "review it" with all the sympathy that I feel for it, for you. You know that anyhow.

What a relief it was when, in my treatment of the modern German novel, I at last arrived at you, after I had wearily and with groans worked my way through Stehr, Strauss, and Hesse, and even Gerhart Hauptmann's ventures in the novel.[3] All that sogginess! It's a ridiculous occupation, literary criticism; between us, I feel a little ashamed of it. No matter how ruthlessly I practice it, what am I doing, having to talk about things, even if only for ten minutes, having to read things for preparation with which I am already finished after the first few pages, which yield me nothing, nothing whatsoever? This man Hesse, for example — after all, he has received the Nobel Prize, and students may well expect me to present him to them. And so I read *Steppenwolf* [1927], which people have praised so highly to me, and looked at *Demian* [1919] and [*Peter*] *Camenzind* [1904] and *The Glass Bead Game* [1943], and a few of the others also. And I come away with the feeling of a poor, oversweetened, flavored pudding, a wavering, jelly-like, lumpy blancmange. This *Steppenwolf* — what a sentimental, self-pitying pulp, without structure, without character, without shape, without the slightest incisiveness, above all without real, thoroughgoing sincerity. And this symbolism, this romantic nonsense, how insipid, how thin and pasted on, and how foolish. And *that* twenty-five years after *Tonio Kröger!* But why should I add insult to injury by talking about this to you? It's sheer rage because I had to read the stuff. Incidentally, the only thing that has lasted between Fontane (who, incidentally, is also wearing thin) and *Buddenbrooks* is good Ricarda's *Ursleu*,[4] unique of its kind, but as moving to me as it once was.

So that is my occupation until February — naturally I pick the raisins out of the cake wherever I can, wander off into social history, ethnology, philosophy of art, linger where the lingering is good, and hurry by all the rest. Likewise in the case of Schiller, about whom a great deal might be said . . . In January come my additional public lectures on the "Crisis of the Individual."[5] Quite a bit of the work is still to be done, and for me it is all far too breathless. But — it brings in some money, I must admit, highly necessary money, and henceforth I shall have to keep at it . . . Incidentally — not to be ungrateful — it has its good moments, moments of effectiveness, of a young person's looking up in astonishment, as if awakening, and such moments are a joy.

It is lovely here — the campus, that is — roomy, country-like, with fine old trees and views down to lakes in the valley, and quite mountainous ravines that enclose the university. My colleagues are pleasant and friendly, especially the physicists, but also my "boss," Victor Lange,[6] who is touchingly concerned about me. I really should have no reason to complain, except that I would so like to go back to my own work for a change. Here, of course, I never get around to it at all.

Several requests: (1) Do you by any chance have a copy of your autobiography[7] to lend me? I found it in the library here, but unfortunately only in English. And I would like to copy some passages from it (especially for the Faust essay),[8] but for that need the German text, which I can obtain nowhere. I would be greatly obliged, and would treat the copy with all due care and circumspection.

(2) One that I have to pass on: the request of the faculty here for a short lecture series or even a single lecture when next you come to the East. What would be your most lenient conditions? Would you care to talk about "the art of the novel"?[9] — something that, incidentally, I myself would like to hear from you some day! (Honorary doctorates are forbidden here by the charter; in spirit they have long ago conferred one on you, they want me to tell you.)

[136]

Finally: (3) The Austrian magazine *Das Silberboot* has approached me and wants to dedicate an issue to me. For this purpose it asks your permission to reprint the kindnesses you wrote about me in the *Deutsche Blätter*.[10] They have already appealed directly to you on this matter, but have received no answer. Seems to have been lost somewhere between California and Switzerland (it was in the summer). Now they have asked me to pass their request on to you. I would be grateful, not only for replies on these matters, but also for an account of how you and Katia are, of your plans and work. All the best to both of you, and to Golo, whom I'd like to hear more about. I'll write him directly soon.

Ever yours,
E. K.

I've got into correspondence with Pree after all. More about that in my next.

1. *Briefwechsel.*

2. "Little Herr Friedemann" ("Der kleine Herr Friedemann"), short story, was first published in 1897; "The Way to the Churchyard" ("Der Weg zum Friedhof"), short story, in 1900; *Tonio Kröger,* novella, in 1903.

3. Hermann Stehr (1864-1940) wrote short stories and novels that were both naturalistic and mystical, notably *Der Heiligenhof* (1918). Emil Strauss (1886-1960) wrote tragic stories of children, notably *Freund Hein* ("Friend Death," 1902), a protest against the educational establishment. Hermann Hesse (1877-1962) was awarded the Nobel Prize for Literature in 1946. Many of his works have been translated into English and are widely read by college students. Gerhart Hauptmann (1862-1946), poet, playwright, and novelist, received the Nobel Prize in 1912.

4. Theodor Fontane (1819-1898), the author of *Effi Briest* (1895) and *Der Stechlin* (1898), was one of Thomas Mann's favorite novelists. Ricarda Huch (1864-1947), the author of *Recollections of Ludolf Ursleu* (1893), in 1933 resigned from the Prussian Academy of Arts in protest against National Socialism.

5. The title is in English in the original letter.

6. Victor Lange (b. 1908), who taught German at Cornell, 1938-1957, was chairman of German Studies, 1945 to 1957, when he went to Princeton.

7. *Lebensabriss* (1930; *A Sketch of My Life* [New York, 1930, 1960]).

8. "Säkularisierung des Teufels" ("Secularization of the Devil"), *Neue Rundschau,* 59 (Spring 1948); in *Verantwortung des Geistes.* See Mann to Kahler, January 6, 1949, note 3.

9. Thomas Mann had already lectured at Princeton on "The Art of the Novel," April 10, 1940.

10. "Erich von Kahler," *Das Silberboot* (Salzburg), 4, No. 6 (1948). See Mann to Kahler, October 7, 1945, note 2.

Mann to Kahler

Pacific Palisades
December 15, 1947[1]

Dear Erich:

How delighted I was with your letter, which confirmed the good news that you will be writing about *Faustus* for the *Neue Rundschau.* What you have already said about it "sits smiling to my heart," and I have no doubt at all that the best and most penetrating things will come from you. I don't know what it is about this book, but I am still close to tears whenever I hear a good word about it. The whole thing is like an open wound, and on top of everything else it is condemned to hurt fellow human beings like Pree and Reisi.[2] I have written them long letters to keep them, if possible, from bitter animosity. The misfortune is that the devil dictated to me the montage technique, which had never been tried quite like this, so that a great deal of reality, intellectual and civil, has been pasted into the painting. By "intellectual" I mean, say, all the passages of literal citation from Nietzsche's Passion[3] or the Shakespeare quotations; by "civil" such vulgarities as exposing the fates of my sisters.[4] Somehow, all this is also connected with the excitement of the book, which shows up in almost every review I have seen. Even so cool a critic as Emil Staiger in the *Neue Schweizer Rundschau*[5] comments that here "a passion is at work which in all probability no one would have had the boldness to predict, given the author's biblical age."

It truly is not an everyday occurence for a man of seventy to write his "wildest" book — the credit, of course, goes to this cozy era of ours. The novel of the era, to the extent that I have been able to do it, at any rate, has been done. But where may the naïve and unreflective epic, the *Adventurous Simplicissimus*[6] of these times, come from? I look vainly around for even the possibility. For the qualities that would equip a young fellow to survive the mess[7] will scarcely make him fit to immortalize it.

I am full of respect and sympathy for the courage with which you are waging the struggle for a livelihood and proving yourself in your new teaching post. The nervous yawn that overcomes you when you treat the most recent German novelists is certainly forgivable, and I trust that you delicately conceal the yawn behind your hand. I myself have never, with the best will in the world, been able to read these Stehrs, Strausses, Kolbenheyers,[8] and the rest of them; and as long as I was living in Germany I had a hard time concealing the fact. Probably I didn't succeed. But I think you are doing Hesse alone an injustice. His is after all a beneficently non-German Germanness, and he has something that I feel to be distantly fraternal. I don't know how I would like *Steppenwolf* today; wisely, I did not look back at it when I wrote about the old fellow for his birthdays. But *Narcissus and Goldmund* [1930] was a fine book, *Demian* also had something that hit the nerve, and in *The Glass Bead Game* a dreamy boldness in the realization of things of the mind appeals to me — a highly conservative boldness, granted, but as a work it belongs among the few venturesome and idiosyncratically great conceptions our whipped and battered age has to offer.

The *Sketch of My Life* — my friend, I have rummaged in the irresponsible disorder of my papers for it, but haven't found it. Possibly I simply no longer have it. Won't you ask Bermann for it — he is back in Old Greenwich [Connecticut].

A lecture at your university — how I would like it! If only I had something to offer again. Tell the gentlemen that I am grateful and touched and will most certainly undertake the visit the moment that I am equipped for it. But it is doubtful whether I shall be traveling at all next year. I have been so much under stress recently that I crave retirement, invisibility, for a protracted spell. I also want to find my way into a new task, or an old one. I have just been reading Barker Fairley's excellent *Study of Goethe*:[9] "He was often able to recover a former mode and complete a work that belonged to the past." I can do that too.

Praiseworthy, buoyant *Silberboot!* It may go ahead and print my kindnesses. If only they were a little less sparse I would be even more pleased.

All good wishes from the entire household.

Yours,
T. M.

1. *Briefwechsel.*

2. Emil Preetorius and Hans Reisiger.

3. The reference is to the parallels drawn between Nietzsche's sufferings from syphilitic paralysis and those of Adrian Leverkühn.

4. Carla Mann (1881-1910) and Julia Mann Löhr (1877-1927) committed suicide.

5. "Thomas Manns 'Doktor Faustus,'" *Neue Schweizer Rundschau,* 15 (November 1947).

6. The great German picaresque novel (1669) of the Thirty Year's War by Hans Jakob Christoffel von Grimmelshausen (1625-1676).

7. Mann here makes an untranslatable pun by giving the English word for "mess" the form of the German word for "Mass."

8. Erwin Guido Kolbenheyer (1878-1962) was the author of philosophical and biological studies, novels, and plays.

9. Oxford, 1947.

Mann to Kahler

Pacific Palisades
March 6, 1948[1]

Dear, good Friend:

I can't tell you, or can tell you only with awkward brevity,
how your essay has moved and pleased me.[2] A few days ago
I broke my shoulder bone in a clumsy fall at someone's
house, and I am still all bandaged. For the first few days I
was pretty miserable, but now it's not so bad.

Your essay is the first discussion of the book that goes far
beyond the ordinary reviews, a study written from a high
vantage point of philosophical criticism that takes in my whole
life and life work, with remarkable perception of its unity.
Honoring the work, it also honors the life, not only on a moral
basis, as effort, but as an existence guided and shaped by an
inner "daimon." So naturally I find your essay deeply gratifying and feel thankful for so much intelligent friendship and
insight.

After having read the essay twice in this form, I look forward with pleasure to seeing it again in print. What stirred
me most, perhaps, were the things you said about the almost
savage directness of the book. That directness kept exciting
me all along, and even now makes me feel as if the novel were
still my own secrets. It startles me that you use the word
"montage," for in my own mind I have used it frequently,
and the idea of montage is in fact one of the premises of the
book.

One might almost think that the final paragraph directed

against certain simple-minded notions regarding my comfort and safety strikes a banal note compared with all that comes before. But in the final analysis, it is by no means a bad idea to set that matter straight, both for the Germans and for people like Döblin.[3]

Thanks, dear friend, and warm regards!

Yours,
T. M.

1. *Letters.*

2. "Säkularisierung des Teufels." A carbon copy of the typescript was found among Mann's literary remains.

3. Alfred Döblin (1878-1957), the novelist, was also for a long time a practicing neurologist. He emigrated to France in 1933, to the United States in 1940, and returned to Germany in 1945 as a colonel in the French army. Acknowledged as a major novelist in Germany, he is best known in the English-speaking world for *Berlin Alexanderplatz* (1929).

Mann to Kahler

Pacific Palisades
March 17, 1948[1]

Dear Erich:

It was very good of you to send a telegram asking about my arm. Thank you, it is already much better; I long ago got rid of the cast and now have it only in a sling. But a good many weeks will pass before I am able to use the arm properly again, for in an adult, to put it mildly, such things don't heal so very fast, in spite of diathermy and massage. And the constant need of help is unnerving — for someone to whom the thought of a valet dressing and undressing one has always been a horror.

I think I shall stay quiet this year and not travel. I was supposed to go to Frankfurt to be the speaker in the Paulskirche,[2] but have pleasantly declined — so pleasantly that the mayor had the letter printed — and now Fritz von Unruh[3] is going; he is in any case completely the right man for the occasion. This time I shall probably not visit the East either, and will make '49, the Goethe year,[4] a year for travel again, also go to Europe if world history, devil take it, permits.

I am looking forward to the publication of your *Faustus* essay as I do to Christmas. Zuckerkandl, too, has written very intelligently and warmly about the music.[5] Embittered Schoenberg insists that I add a note to the effect that the twelve-tone technique is in reality his intellectual property and not the devil's.[6] It will look stupid, but so it must be.

Regards from the two of us to you and yours and Broch. Erika intends to be back here on the 23d. Klaus is in Prague. I am eagerly awaiting his account. I have sent a telegram of sympathy to poor Benes.[7]

Yours,
T. M.

1. Princeton.

2. At the centennial of the meeting of the National Assembly in the Church of St. Paul that marked the beginning of constitutional government in Germany.

3. Fritz von Unruh (b. 1885), a writer of historical dramas, became an active pacifist as a result of his experiences in World War I. He emigrated to France in 1932, to the United States in 1940.

4. The two-hundredth anniversary of Goethe's birth.

5. "Die Musik des *Doctor Faustus*," *Neue Rundschau,* 58 (1948), 203-214. Victor Zuckerkandl (1896-1965), conductor, music critic, and philosopher, was for many years professor at Saint John's College, Annapolis, Maryland.

6. Thomas Mann added a disclaimer at the end of *Doctor Faustus* stating that Arnold Schoenberg, not Adrian Leverkühn, the novel's protagonist, had invented the twelve-tone technique of composing.

7. Eduard Benes (1884-1948), who resigned as president of Czechoslovakia in 1938 and went to the United States, again became president in 1945. In February 1948 he was practically stripped of his power by the Communists and resigned in May.

Mann to Kahler

Dear, good Friend:

Heaven help me, I haven't grumbled or growled at receiving no letter from you on this ordinary 73d birthday. Your magnificent essay in the *Rundschau* was congratulation enough, the finest kind of celebration. That it is to be published in English is one more delight. And that Broch, too, wants to try his hand on *Faustus* stirs me deeply. In Germany hymns are appearing about the book — almost a bit disturbing and *gênant*, "if you see what I mean." But everything, simply everything in the book is apologized for. Against that tendency it does seem advisable for someone to interpose in *Vienna* with a correcting word. I hear that a certain "Fury" there has come out with a slashing attack on the book — the mentality of the "inner emigration." In short, somewhat retarded. An indirect rebuke would no doubt be a good idea.

I spent that Sunday as a simple working day, in the morning writing away at my little legend-novel *The Holy Sinner* (after Hartmann von Aue's *Gregorius auf dem Steine*)[2] and in the evening gave a speech that turned out very well at a peace conference called by the arts-sciences-professions people. The applause simply would not stop; it was a revelation that there are still a great many people who find comfort in the truth.

P. is an ass. I wish I could help him, for he has a hard time of it. But that is just it; he is somewhat too inferior to be allowed to put his oar in.

How different with Werner Richter! Please tell him that I always think of him and his work with true respect and have banished the matter of the letter from my mind. His book on France was again so very good — solid, entertaining work.[3] Of course I ought to have written him. But you know — And before I got back to fiction (even though only in a light vein) I had a long period of melancholy and "hangover" after *Faustus,* with a feeling of "that's over forever."

Everyone here sends warm regards.

Yours,

T. M.

The lapse in regard to Otto III[4] has already been pointed out to me. That will be corrected.

1. Princeton.

2. Hartmann von Aue (b. ca. 1185) was the medieval poet whose *Gregorius auf dem Steine* ("Gregorius on the Stone") was the source of *The Holy Sinner* (1952).

3. *Frankreich von Gambetta zu Clemenceau* (1946).

4. Since Kahler's letter is missing, the significance of the allusion is not clear. In *Doctor Faustus* the fictional city of Adrian Leverkühn's birth is called Kaisersaschern because the ashes of Emperor Otto III were interred there. Presumably Kahler had pointed out some historical slip.

Mann to Kahler

Pacific Palisades

September 14, 1948[1]

Dear Erich:

Today I want to give you briefly some news that may interest you and at least will amuse you. Yesterday a letter came from my old friend Agnes Meyer in Washington. You know, the wife of Eugene. She read your essay on *Faustus* in the *Neue Rundschau* and is extremely enthusiastic about it. I herewith copy what she writes in her best German:

"I am overjoyed that Erich Kahler has published such an intelligent article, entitled *'Säkularisierung des Teufels.'* Please tell him that your best American critic [that's she] maintains that this is the only really insightful study of your works, and that this comes from someone who has probably read everything about you. Adolf Busch[2] has promised that he will arrange for me to meet Kahler. But do tell him that he should simply visit me when and if his way brings him to Washington. It would be a pleasure to talk about you with a person of such intelligence."

Later in the letter she reverts to you once more and says: "It is odd how much courage an article like Kahler's gives me. It makes one see that there are, after all, people who know that what is at stake today is a matter of life or death."

So you see, you have made a deep impression, and I am writing you all this in order not to lag behind Adolf Busch, who has promised to arrange for you to meet this extremely influential and by no means stupid woman. You really shouldn't omit calling on her if something takes you to Washington. Incidentally, since she very frequently goes to New York, I shall write her that it would be more practical to arrange a meeting with you there sometime.

No more for today. The little San Francisco family has left us again until Christmas, and Golo is staying in the vicinity, and Erika, too, is back, They all send their very warm regards, especially the secretary.

Yours,
Thomas Mann

I have just received an excited letter about *Faustus* from a Kurt H. Wolff in Columbus, Ohio. From the writing and the text it *could* be the publisher Kurt Wolff, and then again not. I am altogether confused. Please tell me quickly: does Wolff now live in Columbus?[3]

1. Princeton.

2. See Mann to Kahler, July 8, 1940, note 2.

3. Kurt H. Wolff (b. 1912), German-born sociologist — not the publisher — taught at Ohio State University, in Columbus, Ohio, from 1945 to 1959, and is now at Brandeis University.

Mann to Kahler

Dear Erich:

A happy New Year! How are you, dear friend, and what are you up to? We ask each other that often, and it remains a perpetual pity that we must live so far apart. In the month of May we are thinking of coming again and then proceeding to England and Sweden, and to Switzerland again. German newspapers keep saying that I will be coming to Germany also. But I don't believe a word of it.

In the winter issue of the *Neue Rundschau* you will see the first parts of those recollections of the genesis of *Doctor Faustus* which are to be published as a small book in March.[2] I am somewhat ashamed of this document, which came into being only because inwardly I was unable to detach myself quickly from the book — probably out of the feeling "that's over forever." The reviews here were, of course, predominantly illiterate. The *New Leader* surprisingly intelligent, the *Atlantic Monthly* very good. But naturally your essay has remained the best. Wasn't it supposed to be published in *Commentary?*[3] I keep waiting for that. It is not in the January issue, either. Has the magazine decided otherwise? I know what trouble you had with the translation.

Our house was overpopulated for the holidays. Erika, Klaus, and the grandsons have remained. We old folks are growing older and older, and our heads waggle. At the same time my wife also has much to do looking after old Heinrich, who has moved closer to us. I have done a good deal of writing on *The Holy Sinner* (Gregorius) and am now attacking the lecture on "Goethe and Democracy."[4] It will be highly reminiscent of the old mantelpiece clock I was given for Christmas, on which four shining balls repeatedly go once around to the left and once around to the right.

Warmly yours,
Thomas Mann

1. Princeton.

2. *Die Entstehung des Doktor Faustus*: *Roman eines Romanes* (Amsterdam, 1949) (*The Story of a Novel*).

3. "Thomas Mann's 'Doctor Faustus': 'Terminal Work' of an Art Form and an Era," *Commentary*, 7 (April 1949), 348-357; titled "Secularization of the Devil: Thomas Mann's 'Doctor Faustus,'" in *The Orbit of Thomas Mann*.

4. Presented May 2, 1949, at the Library of Congress, in honor of the two-hundredth anniversary of Goethe's birth.

Mann to Kahler

March 6, 1949[1]

Dear Erich:

I am very glad to have the English translation. It is excellent, and I find that it reads as well as the original, in a way even more easily, because its attitude is less "scholarly." Yet all the depth of the criticism comes through. There are *such* fine passages in it, fine in sheer intelligence! Especially your words about the convergence of the life work, and then again its summation in this book, touch and gladden me again every time. Moreover, it is simply a gratification to me that this essay is being published here just now. You have done me — i.e., the book — a great service. The effect of your essay can only be instructive, also reproving, also shaming. You ought to send it to Harry Levin at Harvard, who has taken such a strangely malicious attitude. For my part, I shall send him the coming little book on the genesis of *Faustus*, in which his book on Joyce[2] is gratefully noted.

From Cornell they write me about how reluctant they were to let you go again.

I am wracking my brains about Germany, Munich. They have appointed me "honorary president" of the new literary academy and want me to speak at an official Goethe celebration. Should I? Shouldn't I? After all, it is the city in which I spent forty years of my life, and visiting it would stand for a visit to the whole of Germany. But I am still wavering irritably. Preetorius keeps insisting in every possible way.

Yours,
T. M.

1. Princeton.

2. Harry Levin (b. 1912), professor of literature at Harvard, who wrote *James Joyce* (Norfolk, Conn., 1941), reviewed *Doctor Faustus* in the *New York Times,* October 31, 1948, p. 5.

Mann to Kahler

Pacific Palisades
September 10, 1949[1]

Dear, good Erich:

Heartfelt thanks for your long, devoted letter. It's a wonder and wonderful how you find the time for such, given the outwardly and inwardly bustling life the letter itself reflects. I cannot repay it well, for I am after all somewhat tired, and in addition unwell from the autumnal heat which has descended here. It unsettles the nerves and stomach, and makes catching cold all too easy. During the trip, I may say, I bore up like a man, but no sooner did I reach home than all the heroism dropped away from me, and I no longer understand how I defied the storm. At the request of the N.Y. *Times Magazine* I wrote a brief, though no doubt still too long, description,[2] but for good reasons I have my doubts that it will be published. Now I am trying to push forward the little Gregorius novel, as merrily as it will go; for four months I did not work at it for a single day (since in Vulpera-Tarasp

[Switzerland] I had to prepare the speech I was to give in Germany).[3] In Frankfurt, at a private party (at Professor Eppersheim's)[4] I read aloud from it and aroused great amusement with the two fishermen on a Norman island who talk a rashly invented dialect made up of English, French, and Low German. Such are the pastimes we devise in our old days. After *Faustus* I cannot really take anything seriously. "That's over forever," Fontane said after *Effi Briest*.

The trip — telling about it would be something for conversation. Part of it was fantastic, and it is really curious to see to what regal situations such a life of play and dream finally leads, when you keep it up long enough. In Germany, it is true, the "regal" aspect consisted chiefly of the hordes of police that the sober Social Democratic city fathers, with their deep sense of responsibility, thought advisable. Those city fathers will be swept away soon enough, and my visit probably took place at the last possible moment. The development in the direction of renazification is running full speed ahead under our protection, and in two years, I think, German honor will be completely restored. You have no conception of the viciousness of the press. I am speaking of the West. In the East (if Thuringia is East) iron discipline naturally prevails — and, just between us two, there can be something pleasant about it. Those people think I can be bribed by flags, garlands, chanting choruses, toasts, and marching town bands. Oh, no. But I might possibly be bribed by the fact that over there I did not read a single abusive letter or stupid sneering article.

But all that is "truly a broad subject," as old Briest says. I am reading the novel again. A masterpiece! The fact that he also wrote *Der Stechlin* after it imposes some kind of obligation.

Warmly yours,
Thomas Mann

[150]

1. Princeton.

2. "Germany Today," *New York Times Magazine,* September 25, 1949.

3. "Ansprache im Goethejahr" ("Address for the Goethe Year"), delivered at the Paulskirche, Frankfurt, July 25, 1949, and at the Nationaltheater, Weimar, August 1, 1949 (*Gesammelte Werke,* XI).

4. Probably Hanns W. Eppelsheimer (b. 1890), professor of literature and the history of ideas; he was director of the city and university library, Frankfurt, 1946-1958.

Mann to Kahler

The Shoreland
Chicago
April 22, 1950[1]

Dear Erich:

Many, many thanks for your letter. We — Erika making a third — have been en route since the 19th, and today I am lecturing here at the university on "The Years of My Life."[2] It is the same lecture I shall deliver in New York in German, under the auspices of *Aufbau,* at the Kaufman Auditorium on Lexington Avenue.[3] We will be staying at the Hotel Carlyle this time; Walter[4] recommended that we do so. We'll not be arriving until the 26th itself, and on May 1 fly on to Stockholm. Our free times will be the *evening of the 27th* and afternoons of the 28th and 29th. So my wife has just informed me! I would never be able to keep that in my head. Send word to us at the Hotel Carlyle directly about when we can see you. We shall not be back until the first half of August, for after the visits in Sweden and Paris we want to have an ample stay in Switzerland.

Warmly,
Yours,
Thomas Mann

[151]

1. Princeton.

2. At the University of Chicago; in *Harper's Magazine,* 201 (October 1950), 250.

3. "Meine Zeit" (*Gesammelte Werke,* XI; "The Years of My Life," *Harper's,* October 1950).

4. Bruno Walter.

Mann to Kahler

Pacific Palisades
February 1, 1951[1]

Dear Erich:

You cannot imagine how it troubles me that I haven't yet thanked you for your friendly season's greetings, or even for your splendid essay in the magazine of the atomic scientists.[2] The essay truly strikes me as written from the depths of my own heart. And really, agonized as we all are by so much falsehood, the ring of truth almost brings tears to the eyes. If only I did not have the feeling that it is all in vain. The good books, the commentators who, rarely enough, still risk a word of warning over the radio — none of that has the slightest influence. Obstinately and inexorably nemesis takes its course, following the vilest laws, and sometimes I catch myself thinking: just as well; let it come the way they insist on having it. Human wickedness deserves a visitation such as the earth has not yet seen — and this civilization of grabbers, fools, and gangsters deserves to perish.

How hard-working you are! Right after the political essay comes this one on aesthetics in the *Rundschau.*[3] It is very rich and fine criticism. And yet I know you must simply have stolen the time to produce these good things.

With my energies plainly dwindling and a sense of depression growing, I have managed to put together nothing but trifles since the summer. A lecture on Shaw for the London

B.B.C.[4] seems, contrary to all expectations, to have been a kind of "hit." In Switzerland an article on Michelangelo's poetry has been published,[5] and here in the *Sat. Review of Literature* one on a collection of Wagner's letters.[6] But since *The Holy Sinner* is out of the way and in print, I have taken up the ancient *Felix Krull*[7] once again and am continuing it, letting him saunter on into the unknown without any real faith that I shall ever finish it. I suspended work on it in 1911 to write *Death in Venice*, and it is truly curious to take up the old fragment again after four decades and all I have done in between. I have actually resumed on the selfsame page of Munich manuscript paper (from Prantl on Odeonsplatz) where I stopped at that time, unable to go on.

God knows whether we shall be coming East in the spring. I no longer have lectures, at any rate, and it would only be a stopover on the way to Switzerland, which as things stand has by degrees and rather without any special grounds become my favorite country, and where I should gladly spend the last brief years of my life. We must see.

Cordially,
T. M.

1. *Letters.*

2. "Foreign Policy Today," *Bulletin of the Atomic Scientists,* 6 (December 1950).

3. "Was ist ein Gedicht?" *Neue Rundschau,* 61, No. 4 (1950).

4. "He Was Mankind's Best Friend," Mann's eulogy on Bernard Shaw, was broadcast twice in January 1951 on the B.B.C.'s Third Program ("Bernard Shaw," *The Listener* [London], January 18, 1951).

5. "Michelangelo in seinen Dichtungen," *Du* (Zurich), 10 (October 1950); in *Altes und Neues* as "Die Erotik Michelangelos."

6. "Wagner without Blue Pencil," *Saturday Review of Literature,* 34 (January 20, 1951), 7-9.

7. *Confessions of Felix Krull, Confidence Man: The Early Years* (1954).

Kahler to Mann

April 14, 1951[1]

My dear Friend:

It is again a long, far too long time that I have owed you my thanks and a letter! Of course there are always plenty of reasons, and all of them of course are ultimately invalid. My mother died in January; although long expected, it was a wrench and a blow, all the more so since up to the last she remained, aside from her deafness, mentally alert. Then here, after the windup of the semester at Cornell, there were all sorts of troubles and tribulations which it would be a bore to tell you about. There is a mountain of work facing me, aside from the two major, ever waiting, and repeatedly interrupted tasks — finally finishing up the book of essays,[2] the revision of a German translation of *Man the Measure* (a veritable nightmare), et cetera, et cetera — and all that in a state of acute depression, under the spiritual pressure of the state of the world and of the ghastly intellectual and moral conditions in which we live here.

Still: I hear, and your letter hints at it, that you are toying with the thought of moving to Europe, to Switzerland. Please don't do it! I cannot help warning you against it. You would gain nothing by it, for there is simply no escaping from what is going to happen this time. If we must suffer here from the delusions of stupid, perverted power, over there we will suffer from the unrelieved illusions of shameful impotence. And if what you fear really should prove to be inevitable, it would catch up with us there as well as here. So why go to all the effort and expose yourself to the harmful and spiteful misinterpretations your leaving would set off in this country? The only place to go that might serve a human, a demonstrative purpose would be India. But of course that would be an excessive imposition upon both of you physically. It seems to me we must stay and resist where we are.

In this connection I must tell you a little anecdote that illustrates our situation. Two friends are crossing the Atlantic, one sailing from Europe to America, the other from America to Europe. In the middle of the ocean the ships meet and pass. The friends standing at the rail recognize one another, and both call across the water simultaneously, "Are you crazy?"

Day before yesterday I again had occasion to hail your *Faustus*. The Department of Literary Criticism here arranged a seminar on the book and asked me to give an introductory lecture.[3] Since it bores me to repeat the same thing, this time I tried to present your *Faustus* as the culmination of all Fausts, or rather as the point of convergence of the history of the motif with the history of your novels, which gave me the opportunity for a comparison (highly attractive to me) of yours with Goethe's *Faust*. I am having it typed and will send it to you, although it offers nothing essentially new, at least not new to *you*. There was an outside audience, and a discussion was held, and I was able to observe how keenly and how seriously people take *Faustus,* especially the young.

I am waiting impatiently for *The Holy Sinner!* When is it due? And how is the *Krull* progressing?

As might have been expected, I did not receive the Guggenheim. I am, of course, too old according to their statutes, long beyond the stage of a "promising young man," and moreover it was altogether stupid of me to hand in this theory of history which their experts regard as useless German philosophizing and as an insult to their existence. I would not even have gone into the whole thing had not Mr. Moe[4] actually invited me to do so, even extending the application deadline for me. But at any rate it is a great pleasure that Golo has received it, and deserves it. I have once again to thank you for a letter of reference. If only these reference efforts were not always linked to such applications!

Please let me have a brief account of your doings! All the best to Katia and Erika.

Ever yours,
Erich

1. Thomas Mann Archives, Zurich.

2. *Die Verantwortung des Geistes.*

3. The manuscript of this lecture is in the Erich Kahler Archive, Firestone Library, Princeton University.

4. Henry Allen Moe (b. 1894), trustee, formerly president, of the John Simon Guggenheim Memorial Foundation, which awards fellowships for advanced studies.

Mann to Kahler

Pacific Palisades
April 23, 1951[1]

Dear Friend:

Thank you for your good, kind letter. And above all, our sympathy for your grief over your mother. "You know, 'tis common . . ." And you were expecting the inevitable. Nevertheless, it is a totally unique shock and wrench, as I very well remember from my own experience. Good that you are so busy and hopeful in so many directions, even though all this furthering, arranging, and building is done under the pressure that weighs so heavily on us all. I know exactly what you mean by "acute depression." I myself am nothing but a bundle of nerves, trembling at every thought and word. Only yesterday I let myself break down and weep listening to the *Lohengrin* prelude — simply in reaction to all the baseness. Have people ever had to inhale so poisoned an atmosphere, one so utterly saturated with idiotic vileness? We live in a world of doom from which there is no longer any escaping. Your "Are you crazy?" anecdote is striking enough, except that in my opinion the man sailing westward is just a trace crazier, for despite the fact that dear Switzerland may be even more pro-American than some Americans, it seems to me that in general the European mentality does not come up to the barbarous infantilism we have here, especially not since the notable turn toward pacifism the Roman Church has taken. It knows why.

For the rest, we are a long way from forming any definite plans. Erika, who is ordinarily the element of practical energy in the house, is much too sick to take any such thing in hand. She had to have a very serious operation, from which she is only slowly recovering. First of all, then, we must wait until she is well. But in other respects too there are so many affairs in suspension: the sale of the property, the purchase by Yale library of my entire "posthumous papers," including diaries I have kept since 1933, for which some uncowed philanthropist must come forward — and other things. The farthest we will go — and Katia prefers this idea — is that we shall rent the house, if possible, for a year and spend that time in Europe, first of all in Gastein [Austria]; the baths attract me because of arthritic-rheumatic difficulties with my hip and arm. But even this temporary step is quite uncertain. It is also a question of money. We know nothing at all.

My Gregorius story has appeared in Germany, and copies have no doubt arrived here by now. Naturally I wanted to send it to you, but at first had so few copies that there were none to spare. A further shipment is en route, and you will receive the little book from me as soon as possible, even if it should come to you meanwhile without my intervention. I can imagine that you may like it. It is full of jokes and parodies a great deal of tradition. But underneath all that, it is very serious about the idea of grace, which has long been a focal point of my thinking and living. After all, isn't it pure grace that after the consuming *Faustus* I was able to bring off this little book of God-sent jests and diversions? Possibly I might bring off still more, say the continuation of the Krull memoirs, of which there is already a sizable heap of manuscript. But I doubt whether mood and strength will be sufficient under the present circumstances.

Cordially,

Yours,
Thomas Mann

1. *Letters.*

Mann to Kahler

Pacific Palisades
June 23, 1951[1]

Dear Erich:

We have thought about you a great deal since the news of Hermann Broch's passing[2] reached us, news that affected even us so strongly. But how sad you must be, and how deserted you must feel. First your mother and now your closest friend. Far beyond the loss to the world of mind that this too early, this lamentable demise means to us all, to society, it must touch you to the quick. Over and above all his already magnificent achievements, what a life full of *promise* has been prematurely cut off! It is very, very painful; and I only wish I were present and could clasp your hands, for you were closest to him and mourn with the greatest knowledge of what has been lost.

I recently had an exchange of letters with old Alvin Johnson,[3] who likewise knew what Broch was, and expressed my willingness to join a group of American intellectuals in proposing him to Stockholm for the Nobel Prize. It would have been a fine, impressive choice, greatly to the honor of the committee. Past.

Since Erika, who was seriously ill, is feeling better, we intend after all to get our Europe trip in this year. Principally I want to go to Gastein to try the cure for my wretched rheumatism. But we also want to stay in Switzerland again. On July 9th we shall be in New York for a single day (St. Regis). Can you arrange to spend that evening with us? We would have no right to be surprised if it doesn't work out, but it would be nice.

The ladies here send their warm regards.

Your old
Thomas Mann

1. *Briefwechsel.*

2. Broch died May 30, 1951, in New Haven, Connecticut.

3. Alvin Johnson (1874-1971), teacher and writer, editor of the *New Republic,* 1917–1923, was director of the New School for Social Research, New York, 1923-1945, which he transformed, during the Nazi years, into a veritable haven for refugees.

Kahler to Mann

Princeton
December 24, 1951[1]

Dear Friend:

Before this baleful year comes to an end I want to write, at last, my long intended and, as usual, postponed letter. It has been in my mind and my heart for months, since Katia's telephone call to Princeton when I missed you for the second time this year — an altogether inexcusable mishap that comes close to being misconduct. The fact that I have not seen you at all this year, when I so particularly needed to, is part of the general and multiple misfortune of this year. It was a regular "current," one of those waves of fate that in an uncanny fashion confirm for us the reality of organic destiny. Such series make us feel even more deeply than sunny periods the significant pattern of our own lives, and for this we must actually be grateful. Nevertheless, I hope that what has happened so far is the end of it, and that the wave will start moving upward again just a little.

Enough of this; perhaps the details can be reported orally sooner or later. It is Christmas and a new year, and for a while the inclination is strong to turn to pleasanter things. Thank God and touch wood, good news has come about you by various routes. *The Holy Sinner* reflected an almost ebullient mood. I recently read it again for my course and for the first time really enjoyed all the sly profundities it is full of. I talked for a good hour in my lecture, though with some circumspection in view of my adolescent audience. Now I am filled with ideas for an extended essay on it, if only time permitted. As always, I have far too many projects afoot and on my shoulders for my well-known caterpillar-like or centipedal mode of progression. Above all there is this nuisance of a German translation, this wretched *Man the Measure*. A German professor has been translating it with great zeal, but with remarkable stylistic and terminological insensitivity, into his professorial language, which I cannot bear to be blamed for. Alas, your well-meant but ominous wish may be fulfilled, that I write the book once again in German, with sizable additions. But at the same time I find it so stale and writhe with impatience to get to altogether different and far more advanced matters. Furthermore, I have other work for a livelihood, must report on manuscripts and bulky books for Bollingen,[2] and so on. On top of all that, I shall not be able to sit down quietly and go to work until my semester at Cornell is over again. Broch's posthumous papers are also giving me a great deal to do. Dear me! I am longing to go to Europe, but once more a trip is out of the question; lack of money is also a factor.

Here I found the new issue of the *Rundschau* waiting for me, with the *Krull* chapters,[3] which I shall not be able to read at leisure until the Christmas commotion is over. But I am happy that this work is thriving, and look forward to more.

Best to say nothing at all about the world. Once again I've made public statements on a few occasions, but what's the use, what's the use? It is talking against walls of regimentation.

It would be good to have a direct word from you again. How is Erika, and where is she? What is Golo doing, the scoundrel? Not only has he failed to come, when I so badly needed his comforting presence; he is also silent, and this time without the slightest justification, since for a change it was *I* who wrote last to him.

But to all of you my deepest, most affectionate good wishes, and may I soon see all of you for a good long spell.

Yours,
Erich

Enclosed, a few views of Beissel's[4] realm, which we went to see on the way home from Virginia.

I have an immodest and in fact shameless request, and even though the pen has actually indicated its reluctance by a blot, I cannot refrain from making it. I gave Fine, who wanted it very badly, the copy of *Young Joseph* which you once dedicated to us jointly, as well as the copy of *The Beloved Returns,* also inscribed to us both. So I now have neither. Unfortunately, *Young Joseph* can no longer be had separately. Would you by any chance have a copy left? That is the immodest request. The shameless one involves a newly inscribed *The Beloved Returns*. Graciously consider it, and if it is too annoying say no.

On the 2d I am returning to Ithaca (112 Sage Place, Ithaca, N.Y.). From February 1 on, I intend to be back here in Princeton.

1. *Briefwechsel.*

2. The Bollingen Series, then published by Pantheon Books, now by Princeton University Press, is sponsored by the Bollingen Foundation. Under a now discontinued program of grants for research and writing, Kahler was a Bollingen Foundation fellow, 1948-1950.

3. "Reise und Ankunft, Circus," *Neue Rundschau,* 62 (November 20, 1951).

4. The composer Johann Conrad Beissel (1690-1768), of Ephrata, Pennsylvania, is described by Kretschmar in *Doctor Faustus.* Thomas Mann's source was Hans Theodore David, "Hymns and Music of the Pennsylvania Seventh Day Baptists," *American-German Review,* June 1943.

Mann to Kahler

January 2, 1952[1]

Dear friend Erich:

Today I took the requested books to the mail. Unfortunately, *Young Joseph* is no longer to be had separately. I had to take this first volume from the three-volume edition of *Joseph.* But at any rate this way you have part of the book twice over, which is better than your not having the first volume, which today I am inclined to regard as the most remarkable and original of them.

Your Christmas Eve letter was a delight to all three of us, and we affectionately return your good wishes for this already slightly nibbled year. What will it bring on the greater scene and in our personal lives? For us possibly, almost certainly, significant changes. It may be unwise at our — my — age to turn our life topsy-turvy once again and place it on a new basis. And yet it is this way: the older I grow, the more obstinately there settles in me the irrational and almost anxious tug and urge to return to the old earth whose son I am and in whose womb I should like to rest some day — not here, not here! Of course I am not speaking of Germany. But if we can sell our house here for a decent price — agents assure us it can be done in a few months — we will not return from our next trip to Europe, but settle permanently in Switzerland, probably in the Tessin. I see the wearisome confusion it will involve, the labors of installing ourselves afresh. But brave Katia is prepared to take that upon herself. And Erika — she is careful not to say a word in favor of the decision but is understandably ardently in favor, since after all this country, with its moronic and persecution-mad atmosphere, smothers her vital personality and every chance she might have to be effective and to keep active. Golo, too, who is over here right now, urges us to take the step.

Please keep all of this to yourself? Our detaching ourselves from America naturally has to be done with the greatest prudence. Without any ostentation, and altogether as if it were a temporary and provisional matter. Technically, it is made possible by the Swiss-American tax agreement which protects American citizens living in Switzerland from double taxation. I have been in correspondence with Bern about that — they speak of being "delighted" and "honored" — at least the Social Democratic Federal Council, to which the Finance Department is subordinate.

Heavens, how busy you are — the German version of *Man the Measure*, the Bollingen reports, the Broch papers — and still full of curiosity about new undertakings! The wave of misfortune you write vaguely about doesn't seem to have got you down. But burdened as you are, I wish someone had made you write on *The Holy Sinner* for the *Neue Rundschau*. How different it would have read from the womanish stuff that now fills those pages. Even Reisiger would have provided something fresher, more stimulating and gratifying. Incidentally, when I wrote the story I was not more ebullient than usual, only more courageous — *somewhat* more than I am now, perhaps, for with the continuation of the *Krull* I have once more burdened myself with something whose demands, in whimsicality and inventiveness, go beyond my years, I fear. At the same time I am again being visited by the tendency to make everything I touch, even something so light, degenerate into the "Faustian" mode and turn into a pilgrimage through infinity. But to whom am I complaining!

Cordially,

Yours,
Thomas Mann

1. Princeton.

Mann to Kahler

Pacific Palisades
June 5, 1952[1]

Dear, good friend Erich:

Your book[2] has given me such pleasure, I have read so deeply in it, and now I can thank you for it only with impoverished, tired words. For some time I haven't been feeling very well (without, incidentally, having any specific reason), and at the same time I am always, as Luther so expressively puts it in a letter (I like to quote the phrase, which certainly applies to you too) "overladen, overcrowded, overwhelmed by affairs." I am longing for Gastein, and our departure, first to Switzerland, is really near. We are flying to Chicago on the 24th. There we shall stay for a few days, and from the afternoon of the 26th to the 29th, when we fly on to Europe, we shall be in New York, Hotel St. Regis. There we do hope to see you this time, so that I can clasp your hand for the gift of your book — unless you yourself precede us to Europe. I have the impression that you had this in mind. Just as well; then we shall meet somewhere over there.

Your book — I simply love its voice, that anguished vibrato which testifies to the distress of heart and mind out of which it was all written, the distress we all share. It testifies also to the compassionate concern of a man whose wisdom might easily have made him scornful and cold, but who continues to concern himself with the fate of poor, poor, stupid, stupid humanity. I was again deeply moved by the magnificent *Faustus* study, profoundly stirred by the birthday article on the "Responsibility of Mind." But everything else is on the same high level, every stirring and, one would imagine, irresistible plea to take thought. Let him listen who has ears to hear! In any case I feel that the existence of such books — the fact that at least they are written — will somewhat save the honor of humanity, if "man" as an experiment should prove to be a mistake refuting the whole of Creation.

See you soon!

Yours,
Thomas Mann

1. *Letters.*
2. *Die Verantwortung des Geistes.*

Mann to Kahler

Dear Erich:

Thank you for the letter from the land of the Brits. I suppose you are now locatable at Pree's. Day before yesterday we arrived here and will stay three weeks (Hotel Viktoria), are then going to Strobl am Wolfgangsee [Austria] and to Salzburg, then (August 20) to Gastein. There we also want to spend three weeks and will then return to the Waldhaus Dolder, Zurich, where we will be staying for a few days between here and the trip to Austria. In the autumn, at the end of September or beginning of October, a journey to Rome is to follow; and what comes then lies hidden in mists, for our California house has not yet been sold, but I do not want to return there. The country makes me altogether ill.

So our programs do not seem to fit one another very well. All the same, we shall be here until the end of July, and the town is a station on the Simplon rail line to Italy. That remark is not intended as an imposition, only a delicate hint.

May you have a happy journey through the protectorate of Germany! It was balm to the spirit that the Danes said, "Nothing doing."[2]

Cordially,

Yours,
Thomas Mann

My regards to Pree.

1. Princeton.

2. Until the autumn of 1952, Denmark did not permit the establishment of air and naval bases on Danish territory by outside forces of the North Atlantic Treaty Organization.

Kahler to Mann

Dear Friend:

Once again I should have written long ago and meant to, and now the final push is given to me by this handsome gift of the essay volume;[2] with pride and joy I see myself figuring in it. Many and special thanks! What a wonderful volume it is. How freely and surprisingly it is yourself, in person, from all sides, in all facets: the grand, far-reaching, earnestly concerned aspects alongside lightness, gracefulness, casualness, into which suddenly, unexpectedly, a total surprise within the context itself, slips something deeply stirring! The richness, the superabundance of the collection is tossed off with the ease that a writer attains only from the summit of a great opus. And a whole generation — how much of my own life also! — moves with you through the book. I have been strolling in it evenings and at night, full of memories, deeply moved, recollecting, with you and with myself. And sometimes I must pause in amazement: To think of all the things we have been through, and what a miracle that we have survived it all up to this point!

Medi was here for three days, on the way to Chicago with her charming devils[3] — it felt so good to have her here once again after such a long time and to see her without tension and burdens. Though she did seem pretty well worn out, the poor child. She spoke of your having been unwell and out of sorts, but, thank God, Bermann came soon afterward and gave an entirely different report, of Cambridge and Munich and your histrionic successes and of the sensational audience with the pope.[4] How did that come about, and did you go so far as to have pontifical "shop talk" about *The Holy Sinner* with him?! It made me very happy to hear that *Krull* is

[167]

finished and so successful; I look forward to it with great eagerness, and also to the continuation of the novella, which I began reading in the *Merkur*.[5]

Things are getting worse and worse here — but that you are well aware of over there, and, thank God, Europe is beginning to stir against it a little. What can be done here in civil liberties emergency committees and similar groups (in which I have been doing my best) remains quixotic drudgery. What is to be done, where should we turn? I had quietly hoped to get away for a while, had an invitation from the University of Manchester for a year. They applied to Fulbright for me, since they connot pay for it by themselves; but as might have been expected, I was refused the Fulbright (non-American and I suppose un-American also). A year ago, when I was issued my passport, Einstein said to me, "You ought to be ashamed!" Now I can face him again, to some extent.

I suppose there is scarcely any "escape" for me. In Switzerland there is no way for me to earn a livelihood. In Germany I could probably obtain a "position" nowadays, but in spite of that temptation, above all the level of the students, I cannot feel at ease in that country. Now party uniforms are again permitted, and the game of "protecting the meeting halls" can soon begin anew! A lecture series, that would be possible; but returning there entirely — no, no. So I shall probably have to stick it out here.

As for my writing, after several literary things (you surely have my essay in the *Rundschau*)[6] I have turned back to history and intend, gaily jumping such hurdles as occasional pieces, lectures, etc., to continue on this course for a while.

Please let me have a little personal news from you, and accept my warmest good wishes in advance for your birthday, and for Katia and Erika.

Ever yours,
Erich

1. *Briefwechsel.*

2. *Altes und Neues.*

3. Angelica and Domenica Borgese.

4. In April 1953, Pope Pius XII received Thomas Mann in a private audience.

5. *Die Betrogene, Merkur,* May–July, 1953; *Die Betrogene* (Frankfurt, 1953) (*The Black Swan* [New York, 1954]).

6. "Untergang und Übergang der epischen Kunstform," *Neue Rundschau,* 64, No. 1 (1953).

Mann to Kahler

London
June 5, 1953[1]

Dear Erich:

Your letter arrived just before our flight, and in Erlenbach there was again no time to thank you for the pleasure you have given me. Now above all I am glad of the chance to congratulate you on your splendid essay in the *Neue Rundschau.* A magnificent piece of work. I definitely must reread it.

I was deeply impressed by Rome, which I had not seen for decades. The millennia-old perspective of Europe that opens out to one there aroused a melancholy pride in me. The climax of the stay was the private conversation with Pius XII, which was arranged in short order. He was exceedingly cordial, but still looked tired from the virus infection he had had at about the same time as myself. "The sickness," he said, "all very well. But the cure!" I understood perfectly, for the injections they give you are taxing in themselves. In general I had the impression that he particularly enjoys recalling his years in Germany, which were evidently the best period of his life. We talked about the Wartburg; looking up at it, so the mayor of Eisenach told me, he had said, "That is a

[169]

blessed castle." Certainly a remarkable pronouncement for a Catholic prince of the Church. I reminded him of that, and we philosophized a bit about the unity of the religious world — in this he was merely being, I suppose, conciliatory toward the unfortunate Protestant, who, by the way, bent his knee before this white figure, who embodies so much, without the slightest qualm.

Then yesterday in Cambridge (a charming town; do you know it?) we received our honorary doctorate together with Nehru,[2] for whose sake Churchill postponed the prime minister's conference till the afternoon. I was very glad to see Nehru again (our first meeting was in San Francisco). He is the best, the wisest, the most understanding of men, and of course he gave the impression of being full of cares.

From here we go to Hamburg day after tomorrow and two readings at the university and the Goethe Society. I won't be able to carry it off without an address to the students,[3] and that is difficult and delicate. But I have more or less worked out the general framework.

Then, after all the *festivitas,* there must really follow a long period of monotonous everyday life, the only proper and fruitful kind of life — insofar as there can still be any question of fruits.

A thousand good wishes! You will need them, I think. Katia sends her warm regards.

Yours,
Thomas Mann

1. *Briefwechsel.*

2. Jawaharlal Nehru (1889-1964) was prime minister of the republic of India, 1950-1964.

3. "Ansprache vor Hamburger Studenten," *Das Nebelhorn* (Hamburg), 1 (June 12, 1953).

Mann to Kahler

Erlenbach-Zurich
January 2, 1954[1]

Dear Erich:

Please, there is no need of apologies! We can very well imagine your position, pressures, and problems; and I for one always have on my lips old Briest's "I know, I know." After all, I too might have written once in a while — had I found the energy to do so. But recently I have been working ridiculously hard to push these Krull memoirs on to a specific point. You see, I would like to cast off one volume, a Part One of them, and let that "see the light," as I once did with the *Joseph* when there was enough manuscript at hand. That will do me good, and I shall see whether people do not think these jests too much beneath my years. In that case I would write no further on it, and think of something more dignified to do.

I am sorry to hear about the aftereffects of your infection, but there too the "I know" applies. With advancing years I have become more and more "receptive" to that sort of nuisance. At the moment I am going around with a boil on my right lower eyelid, and must see the doctor daily. He is very anxious and gives me a great deal of penecellin [sic] (I never know how to spell the word). I can scarcely read and scarcely write. Meanwhile, during the period I was concentrating on the novel, my epistolary debts mounted madly — impossible to get through. Moreover, our thoughts and powers of decision are taken up with everyday concerns, problems of dwelling, for where we are isn't the right place; it is too constricted, too limited, though the situation is beautiful. We were almost on the point of turning to the Vevey-Montreux area and went there repeatedly. But it is too dreary there, and I am attached to Zurich. So we are about to buy a roomy house in the vicinity[2] — a matter of heavy responsibility. We shall have to "put something into it" for refurbishing, repairing, small changes, so in spring there will probably be another lengthy hotel intermezzo before the longed-for final shelter and fixed order are established. No saying whether we'll be able to find time for the planned trip to sunnier climes, Madeira or Teneriffe. It certainly would be good to escape the gray, icy winter here for six or eight weeks. On the other hand, I rather shudder at the prospect of traveling.

Your warning against the edition of Broch's posthumous novel has sunk in;[3] I was in my case not feeling too happy about its publication. Rhein-Verlag sent me the proofs even before Christmas, and wanted some words of recommendation. I refused and asked for more time. Now I have the finished book. From the expertly tossed-off afterword by Stössinger,[4] a clever hack, it is apparent that the book has been cooked up from three different versions, with slight additions by Stössinger. The idea of reading it is extremely repugnant to me — when I don't even know whether I'm reading Broch or Stössinger and whether Broch would have consented to its being read this way. If even the title is arbitrary and misleading, how can we trust it enough to begin reading? On the other hand, I tell myself that these posthumous papers must be included in the collected works in some form or other. Otherwise how could they be made available to scholars? The matter perplexes me; I do not know what attitude to take, and would welcome a more precise opinion from you, *if possible*.

As for Lübeck, you can find it in my anniversary lecture, "Lübeck as a Way of Life and Thought" (in *Altes und Neues*). In addition there are *Buddenbrooks* and the late allusions in *Faustus*. At the moment I cannot think of any specific books on the history and social history of the city and the Hanse.[5] The lady will probably do best to apply to the Lübeck City Library. I can also give her a private address: Dr. Hans

Bürgin, Kappeln a.d. Scheli, Mühlenstrasse 11. He is a Lübecker who has done a bibliography of my things and will certainly be able to give her information.[6]

Golo is living in Zurich, writing two books[7] and editorials for *Die Weltwoche,* and often comes to dinner. Bibi[8] is giving concerts in Toyko and also intends to go to India. His boys, who attend a boarding school in Bern, are at the moment with us for the holidays. After them, Medi will soon be coming with her two wild little ladies.

Don't you think you should be making Antaean contact with the old soil again?[9] You can write here too — perhaps better.

Now my eye overflows.[10]

Yours,

Thomas Mann

1. *Briefwechsel.*

2. The purchase was not made.

3. See Kahler to Mann, January 8, 1954.

4. Felix Stössinger (1889-1954), a journalist and publicist, was a contributor to the *Neue Schweizer Rundschau* and Swiss correspondent for *Aufbau* (New York).

5. The Hanse, or Hanseatic League, was an association of free Germanic cities, including Lübeck, Hamburg, and Bremen; it reached the height of its power in the fourteenth and fifteenth centuries.

6. Hans Bürgin (b. 1904) is the author of the bibliography *Das Werk Thomas Manns* (1959).

7. *Vom Geist Amerikas: Eine Einführung in amerikanisches Denken und Handeln in zwangzisten Jahrhundert* (1954) and *Deutsche Geschichte des neunzehnten und zwangzigsten Jahrhunderts* (1958; *The History of Germany since 1789,* 1968).

8. Michael Mann.

9. In Greek mythology, Antaeus was a Libyan giant, the son of Poseidon and Gaea (Earth), who was long invincible in wrestling because every time he touched the earth, his mother, his strength was renewed.

10. Mann whimsically alludes to his sore eye with a line from Goethe's poem *Der König in Thule.*

Kahler to Mann

Ithaca
January 8, 1954[1]

Dear Friend:

Thank you for your good letter and the information. I have already referred the girl to the pertinent places in your works (and especially the Lübeck essay in the new volume of essays) and to the places in Klaus's and your brother Viktor's books.[2] Her plan started from *Buddenbrooks* itself. But the name you give me will be very valuable to her.

I am glad to supply the explanation you ask for concerning Broch's *Bergroman*, the more so since I gather that you had already smelled a rat without my saying anything. There are three versions:[3] a complete one that Broch had rejected and let lie unpublished for many years — he was right, for in spite of all the beauty and, in fact, the magnificence of the conception, the fundamental lines of this version were still perilously unclear and the book could be misinterpreted and wrongly used. The second version, which was the most successful, is unfortunately broken off in the middle. All the faults of the first are corrected in it, the construction is clearly and vigorously worked out, and above all the contrast between the "white mysticism" of the grand, wise old peasant woman and the "black mysticism" of the demagogic enchanter (to clarify this I must refer to the passage about the *Bergroman* in my introduction to the volume of poems, pp. 35 ff.).[4] In this second version many details are also changed for the better, and a great deal that is new and creatively wonderful is inserted. The third version, finally, which Broch was working on when he died, does not add much; it was chiefly a matter of cutting and tightening up. The "clever hack" — under the aegis of the publisher, whoes intellectual and artistic background is not what it might be and who in this case is being extremely commercial-minded — has "blended" these three versions, and to make matters worse, without precise textual references; he now boasts of having put the novel into "final" form. I have not yet had a chance to check the results, but on principle alone I protested from the start against this improper way of editing posthumous works. Unfortunately my protests were in vain. The only conscientious form of publication — which I advised — would have been to print the first and second versions successively in a single volume. They are different enough to arouse independent interest, would have constituted a highly attractive [one word is illegible] "work in progress" showing how an artist's intentions are carried out. But the publisher wanted to use the book to reap a popular success for Broch. Perhaps he will even succeed, at the expense of the authenticity of the work. The sensational theme and the beauty of the details cannot be killed; the fractures, on the other hand, the subtle discrepancies of structure in the different versions, in so complex a book can be detected only by a very conscientious reader.

For the same reasons, because it wasn't "catchy," the only existing authentic title, and a very lovely and significant one — "Demeter and the Enchantment" — was sacrificed and replaced by a stupidly invented title. For two years I have had the most unpleasant disputes with this publisher and can consider myself lucky to have been able to bring my own edition of the volume of poems safely through all perils. I could not prevent the manipulation of *Bergroman*. The theoretical works are, thank God, in the good hands of Hannah Arendt.[5] (The manuscripts are all preserved in the Yale library, so at any rate are available to scholars.)

Please treat what I have said here *confidentially,* and if you should take any public position, refer solely to the book itself and to what is apparent from the afterword. In this connection my name could only be harmful and diminish the effect of any statement. On the other hand, I cannot refrain from calling the attention of influential friends to what has happened here, for the sake of protecting the dead poet who cannot defend himself and for general pedagogical reasons. Where will it end if such methods of treating posthumous works are allowed? What I would like would be for some intelligent critic to take up the matter on his own and describe what has been done. I very much hope one such will turn up.

But you ought to read the book in any case. It is altogether different from Broch's other books and, as I've said, whatever Stössinger may have done with it, he cannot have ruined its extraordinary qualities, above all the wonderful intertwining of nature in all the events. And I am eager to know what you think of it.

1. This letter, in the form of a first draft, was found by Mrs. Alice Kahler among Erich Kahler's papers in 1972, two years after his death.

2. Viktor Mann (1890-1949), the youngest of three brothers, an adviser to a land bank, was the author of *Wir waren fünf: Bildnis der Familie Mann* (1949; "We were Five: Portraits of the Mann Family").

3. Suhrkamp Verlag finally published all three versions fifteen years after the date of this letter: *Bergroman* (Frankfurt, 1969).

4. Hermann Broch, *Gedichte*, ed. Erich Kahler (Zurich, 1953).

5. Hermann Broch, *Essays,* ed. Hannah Arendt (2 vols.; Zurich, 1955). Hannah Arendt (b. 1906), German-born author and political scientist who came to the United States in 1941, has taught at several universities and is the author of many books, including *The Origins of Totalitarianism* (1951), *Eichmann in Jerusalem* (1964), and *On Violence* (1970).

Mann to Kahler

Sils Maria, Engadine
Hotel Waldhaus
August 12, 1954[1]

Dear friend Kahler:

It troubles me that I haven't written you for so long. You

know how it is: work, affairs, all sorts of minor illnesses, and added to that, the more and more frequent weariness of my years. Oh well. Your letter of the middle of June is here, with the account of your sickness, the operation, and what it has cost you to recover. Although I went through a similar thing when I too was seventy, these lung operations are, I think, the most pleasant kind. Once the decision to operate was taken and carried out, I actually did not experience the time in the hospital as a period of suffering, and quickly and effortlessly cleared out. A kidney affair such as yours is undoubtedly much nastier, and I have the impression that you were unfortunately subjected to a grueling trial of patience. But it's a relief to know that you are on the way to recovery, in fact by now must certainly have your full strength back — and that despite your rashness in burdening your convalescence with the McCarthy hearings![2] Yes, my friend, what is there to say about them? I don't mean only that performance, but the whole thing. One sits mute between the stools. Such is the situation of every decent person today, and all the frothy nonsense one has to swallow in silence is not exactly good for the kidneys. But we go on living out our day, which after all is already reassuringly reddening in the west, and wish the best for those who will have to keep on with it a while longer.

Since finishing the Krull memoirs — as far as they go for the time being (440 pages) — I have done very little. The moving and setting up house were partly to blame for the lack of production. But the house is excellent, spacious and comfortable, with a lovely view of the lake and mountains; it takes only ten minutes by car to be in the city, and on the other hand we are immediately out in the country, among cows and in the woods. I so much hope you will be able to visit us here soon. All sorts of fellow countrymen are coming over from the American universities; Marcuse[3] was here too, and up here Sils Maria is swarming with Professors Auer-

[177]

bach[4] and Stern,[5] to be pronounced Störn. In addition Hesse is here; we have nice evening chats with him.

In the corner of my Californian sofa, which I have been able to set up again (there was no room for it in Erlenbach), I have written the introduction to an American edition of Kleist's stories (Criterion Books)[6] — quite nice, I think. After that, primarily for Russia, a longish essay on Anton Chekhov (d. 1904)[7] — also pretty good. But that is about all. I don't feel like working any more on *Krull* before I find out whether what I have done so far has any appeal. Probably people will think these jests beneath my years. I am even a little embarrassed toward the author of the "Säkularisierung des Teufels." And yet here and there you will extract one thing or another from the book. It is to be published in September.

Now I am already beginning to think, as far as the strenuous air up here permits, about the festival speech I am to deliver next May at the official Schiller celebration.[8] I could not refuse that, impossible though the task really is. It has to be attacked naïvely and personally, and I must try to pour into it something of the glorious magnanimity and the enormous intelligence of the poet and his work. The combination of intellectual pride and the popular touch is almost unique.

I have just been reading a nineteenth-century thing on his burial and the fate of his bones — an utterly scandalous affair which Goethe allowed to take its course without lifting a finger. And even twenty years later when the skull, dug up with much toil out of the refuse (it remains doubtful whether it was the right one), was buried at the Grand Ducal Library in the base of Dannecker's[9] bust of Schiller, Goethe was not present. He sent August.[10] He was always unwell whenever anything was happening that might stir him to too much emotion. I should not be reproached for having called attention, in *The Beloved Returns,* to the ludicrous element in his majesty.

Not, incidentally, that Schiller was entirely unridiculous. But in a certain sense he was "greater," more largehearted than his friend, and Goethe knew it, too.

I was so happy to hear that you will be taking in dear old Helen Lowe! She is looking forward to the feeling of being sheltered in your house, and now after all wishes, almost longs, to translate the *Krull*. But I don't know whether Knopf can be persuaded. She is after all very, very feeble with age. On the other hand, she is the only one who can translate certain passages of the book, verses, doggerel, and altogether strike the tone. I don't know what to advise. Possibly the assignment has already been made.[11]

Do you know a Professor Erich Heller[12] of the University of Wales? He is supposed to write a book[13] for Secker & Warburg for my eightieth birthday, and has sent me an extraordinarily clever volume of essays, *Enterbter Geist*[14] (Suhrkamp), which together with essays on Goethe, Burckhardt, Nietzsche, Rilke, Kafka, and Kraus[15] also contains a piece "From Hanno Buddenbrook to Adrian Leverkühn" — critically interesting, half flatteringly negative. I would be curious to hear your opinion of it.

My wife and Erika, who is with us, send warm regards.

Yours,

Thomas Mann

1. *Letters.*

2. Joseph R. McCarthy (1909-1957), United States senator, 1947-1957, was head of the Permanent Investigating Subcommittee, 1953-1954, whose hearings — televised in 1954 —on Communist activities in government aroused much controversy.

3. Ludwig Marcuse (b. 1894), writer, theater critic, and professor of philosophy and German literature, emigrated to the United States in 1939.

4. Erich Auerbach (1892-1957), who had been professor of Romance languages at Marburg, 1929-1935, taught at Yale University from 1950 until his death.

5. Unidentified.

6. Thomas Mann, "Kleist and His Stories," in Heinrich von Kleist, *"The Marquise of 0" and Other Stories*, trans. Martin Greenberg (New York, 1960).

7. "Chekhov," trans. Tania and James Stern, in *Last Essays*.

8. For the one-hundred-fiftieth anniversary of Schiller's death Thomas Mann gave an address, May 1955, in Stuttgart and Weimar ("On Schiller," in *Last Essays*).

9. Johann Heinrich von Dannecker (1758-1841) was court sculptor at Württemberg and a friend of Schiller and Goethe. Among his best-known works are busts of Schiller and Gluck.

10. Goethe's son.

11. *Felix Krull* was in fact translated by Denver Lindley.

12. Erich Heller (b. 1911), professor of German literature at Northwestern University since 1960, had emigrated in 1939 from Prague to England, taught at Cambridge and Swansea, was guest professor at Hamburg, Harvard, Heidelberg, etc.

13. *The Ironic German: A Study of Thomas Mann* (London, 1958).

14. *The Disinherited Mind: Essays in Modern Literature and Thought* (Cambridge, Eng., 1952).

15. Jakob Burckhardt (1818-1897) was the Swiss historian of art and culture whose best-known work is *The Civilization of the Renaissance in Italy* (1860). Rainer Maria Rilke (1875-1926) was one of the foremost German lyric poets, as well as a writer of prose works. Karl Kraus (1874-1936) was the Austrian essayist and poet whose satirical review, *Die Fackel,* attacked hypocrisy and intellectual corruption.

Mann to Kahler

Kilchberg, [Switzerland]
June 16, 1955[1]

Dear friend Erich:

It was a fantastic, breathtaking turmoil, and I still don't see how I can ever work my way out of the mountain of owed thanks — even with the aid of a printed card. I must write you at once, for your contribution to the birthday issue of the *Rundschau* (which I have not yet been able to read through;

far from it) on *The Holy Sinner*[2] is simply too fine and good of you. My heartfelt thanks for the trouble that you, who are busy in so many directions, have gone to, and with so much artistic success, to give me pleasure. And today I cannot say much more than that, for my state is — you won't believe it, and I have so much work I don't know where my head is. The world seems to have driven itself mad by its own publicity, and is only slowly settling down. There was an alarming feeling that my life is engaged in a kind of solemn dissolution. May it once more compose itself in sedate and creative tranquillity, forgotten by the world!

I was most pleased by two things: an astonishing "Hommage de la France à T. M." — greetings, congratulations, whole essays from all the noted French writers, headed by celebrated statesmen such as Auriol, Herriot, Schuman, Mendès-France[3] — and the fact that the Federal Institute of Technology here conferred an honorary degree of Doctor of Natural Sciences upon me. New, original, and amusing.

In general Switzerland was touchingly attentive, led by Federal President Petitpierre,[4] who came to the celebration in the Conrad Ferdinand Meyer house in Kilchberg, where he delivered a speech in German with the most moving French accent. I shall also, between the two of us, very soon become a Swiss, in disregard of time and order. The township of Kilchberg needs only federal consent, which seems assured.

All my good wishes to you, dear friend!

Yours,
Thomas Mann

1. Princeton.

2. "Die Erwählten," *Neue Rundschau,* 66, No. 3 (1955).

3. Vincent Auriol (1884-1966) was the first president of the Fourth Republic, 1947-1957. Edouard Herriot (1872-1957) was president of the National Assembly, 1947-1954. Robert Schuman (1886-1963) was premier of France, 1947-1948; foreign minister, 1948-1952. Pierre Mendès-France (b. 1907) was premier, 1954-1955.

4. Max Petitpierre (b. 1899) was a member of the Bundesrat (federal parliament of Switzerland), 1944-1961; president of the Confederation, 1950, 1955, and 1960.

Mann to Kahler

Cantonal Hospital
Zurich
August 5, 1955[1]

Dear, good friend Erich:

It touched me deeply that in spite of sickness, operation, and overwork you managed this lovely, charming birthday letter. Did I by any chance send you a card of thanks with a few added personal words? I hope so. In any case, I want to thank you once more for your kind remembrance and to assure you that I am looking forward, as is Katia, with warm pleasure to your visit to Europe and a reunion in Kilchberg in September. By then, heaven help me, I will be back on my feet again and at home, tediously protracted though this illness always is by nature.

My experiences have been strange since I received your letter. I sturdily withstood the Schiller travels in May and then the birthday commotion in Kilchberg and Zurich, and afterward, at the beginning of July, the ceremonials in Amsterdam and The Hague too. Probably I was helped along by the psychological lift that came from receiving the star of a commander of the high Order of Orange-Nassau. I was still quite well when I paid friendly Queen Juliana a visit of thanks at her summer residence. I went there from my beloved Noordwijk, where we had settled in the familiar Huis ter Duin; and I had two enjoyable weeks there, doing light work mornings in my beach hut. Suddenly there was something wrong with my left leg, which I thought was rheumatism, so that I wanted just to limp around ignoring it. But K. consulted a rheumatism specialist there, who declared at first sight that this was not in his province at all, but was a circulatory disturbance, an inflammation of the veins, and the proper person to consult, urgently consult, was the specialist in internal medicine at the University of Leiden. He then came, and confirmed the diagnosis. In fact the leg was twice as thick as the other; but who ever thinks of comparing the thickness of his legs? He recommended that I be taken back as fast as possible by ambulance to Zurich and here, which was done; and now I am lying with alcohol compresses and have to keep to absolute bed rest, vexed by all the previously unknown implications of that state, of which for decency's sake I shall mention only the itching eczema, brought on by the continuous bed warmth, on all possible parts of the body. It certainly is a cross to bear, and a first-class trial of patience. But patience happens to be my strong suit, and the care is actually most accurate and conscientious, under the direction of famous Professor Löffler,[2] a kind of medical prima donna wih a sunny disposition, who leaves it to his chief resident to correct annihilatingly the optimism he radiates: "Certainly. But you see, this thigh is still three centimeters thicker than the other."

Still, only three. I am making progress and in the afternoons already spend half an hour in the armchair, listening on a borrowed phonograph to Mozart, who is the latest object of my interest as an artistic personality. Imagine, he had no feeling at all for nature or architecture and other sights. He did not want to see anything at all, and repeatedly drew his inspirations from music alone — a kind of filtering and aristocratic inbreeding, antipopular like Goethe. Einstein has written very well on the matter.[3]

Keep well and *auf Wiedersehn!*

Yours,
Thomas Mann

1. *Briefwechsel.*

2. Wilhelm Löffler (b. 1887) was director of the medical clinic of the Cantonal Hospital, Zurich, 1937-1957.

3. Alfred Einstein (1880-1952), musicologist and critic who emigrated to the United States in 1933, wrote *Mozart* (1945).

Kahler's Last Letter to Katia Mann

Princeton
Christmas 1969[1]

My dearest Katia:

I did not write after poor Erika's death,[2] although I was very heavy-hearted. Nor do I have any excuse other than that writing has become hard for me, that it is growing harder and harder on such occasions. The obituaries of close and dear persons mount up at my age — two other friends died at about the same time; there is a temptation to write the obituary of our entire world. But the closer and truer and more special the losses are, the closer we ourselves approach the limit of life, the more vapid all consolations sound. Should I say that long, hopeless suffering with a remnant of consciousness is one of the cruelest possibilities of nature, and that to watch it with fortitude is an almost unendurable psychic demand and strain? Ought I to praise her and say what each of us has experienced for himself, that she was a brave, lovely, charmingly vital person, always living at the top of her bent? To say such things to you would seem to me needless and feeble. Yet I may be wrong there.

The prospect of the Thomas Mann Archives' publication[3] gives me great pleasure. I have now reread our correspondence, and relived from this distance in time all our cares and the heavy grief of those years. And yet who would have thought then that it was all merely the prelude to the widespread world atrociousness we have to go along with today.

[184]

With regard to that in particular, publication today seems to me not unimportant; in fact, a broader basis would be desirable. And I would therefore like to ask your support in urging Wysling[4] to accept my proposal that the correspondence be published uncut.[5] I would gladly be prepared to bear the costs of such an expansion.

For the rest, I hope very much to be able to greet you here on this wretched continent soon and for as long as possible.

Give Golo my regards — I miss him very much — and Medi, if she is already with you to fetch you. Tell her that J. has sent us a holiday telegram. Very kind of him.

Lili[6] was so glad to have that talk with you over the telephone in Zurich. She sends her regards and all good wishes.

So, we shall be talking soon!

Ever yours,

E.

1. Copy supplied by Katia Mann.
2. Erika Mann died after a long illness in August 1969.
3. Of the Mann-Kahler letters in *Briefwechsel*.
4. Hans Wysling, editor of *Briefwechsel* and director of the Thomas Mann Archives in Zurich.
5. In the present volume all the surviving letters written by Thomas Mann and Erich Kahler are published.
6. Alice Kahler, the wife of Erich Kahler.

Katia Mann to Kahler

Kilchberg
June 30, 1970[1]

Dear Erich:

January has flashed by and I still have not thanked you for your Christmas letter. But a mountain of unanswered mail constantly oppresses me, and my capacity and energy are low.

It was a hard and totally unexpected affliction; the only "good" thing about it was that Erika evidently was not aware of her condition for a moment, had no pain at all, and so, slowly, very slowly, faded away until on August 27 she passed on without a struggle. It is terribly sad that she is no longer here, and I cannot reconcile myself to this violation of the natural sequence. Moreover, I am myself so amazingly healthy; when the doctor did his routine checkup he had nothing at all to chide me for. Certainly advanced age (something I never wished for) brings with it constantly increasing loneliness. You are fortunate still to have a life companion! I think you are almost the only friend of my generation I still have; and it can never be exactly the same relationship with those who are younger, even if they are one's own children. In principle Golo lives in Kilchberg, but he has many occasions to be away. You know him, of course, and miss him. He is a deeply intelligent, deeply honorable and productive person. The planned trip to America has, after all, been canceled; I lacked the enterprising spirit for it. Perhaps I will manage it in the autumn. Now, in the spring, the children are all coming. Bibi has had the great good fortune to find Gret and, so it seems to me, pretty much the right course for him. Our Medi probably has the happiest disposition of all the children, with her intelligence and her activity, but she has her problems too. I'd rather not talk about the world's problems — there would be no end to that. How the people in our "latitudes" find the high spirits for carnival pleasures, such as we are daily shown on television — it is really hard to understand.

It would be lovely if the year brought a reunion after all. That is my heartfelt wish. Warm regards, to your wife too.

Ever yours,
Katia

1. Copy supplied by Alice Kahler.

Index

[188]

Einstein, Alfred, 183, 184n
Elektra (Hofmannsthal), 38n
Enterbter Geist (Heller), 179
Entstehung des Doktor Faustus, see *Story of a Novel, The*
Eppelsheimer, Hanns W., 150, 151n
Eppersheim, Professor, *see* Eppelsheimer, Hanns W.
Erich Kahler (Eleanor Wolff), 67n
Erich Kahler Archive, 156n
"Erich von Kahler" (Mann), 101, 102n, 137, 138n
"Erotik Michelangelos, Die" (Mann), 153n
"Erwählten, Die" (Kahler), 180, 181n
"Europe, Beware" (Mann), 12n, 22n
Euryanthe (Weber), 77

Fairfield, Cicely (Rebecca West), 78
Fairley, Barker, 140
Falke, O. von, 25n
Faust, 88n, 155; see also *Doctor Faustus*
Faust (Goethe), 57, 67n, 155
Felix Krull, see *Confessions of Felix Krull, Confidence Man*
Fine, *see* Kahler, Fine
Fish, Hamilton, 40, 41n
Fontane, Theodor, 135, 137n, 150
Force and Freedom (Burckhardt), 66-67n
"Foreign Policy Today" (Kahler), 152, 153n
"Forms and Features of Anti-Judaism" (Kahler), 26, 30n
Forty Days of Musa Dagh, The (Werfel), 78n
Franck, James, 116n, 117-118, 120
Frank, Bruno, 32, 33n, 44, 70, 71n, 73, 77, 102, 103n
Frank, Leonhard, 82, 84n, 89, 102
Frankl, Paul, 127, 129n, 130
Frankreich von Gambetta zu Clemenceau (Richter), 144, 145n
Freischütz, Der (Weber), 77

Freund Hein (Emil Strauss), 137n
Frido, *see* Mann, Fridolin
Friedrich, Kasper David, 126, 129n
Friedrich von Gentz, see *Secretary of Europe*

Gaea, 173n
Gauss, Christian, 111, 116n
Gedichte (Broch), 75n, 176n
Gentz, Friedrich von, 40, 41n; see also *Secretary of Europe*
George, Stefan, vii, xi, 7n, 129n
"German Problem, The" (Kahler), 80, 81n
Germans, The, xi, xii, 6n
"Germany and the Germans" (Mann), 96
"Germany Today" (Mann), 149, 150n
Geschlecht Habsburg, Das, vii, 4
Gide, André, 109n
Glass Bead Game, The (Hesse), 135, 139
Gluck, Christoph Wilibald von, 180n
Goethe, August von, 178, 180n
Goethe, Johann Wolfgang von, 7, 29, 91n, 143, 148, 173, 178, 179, 180n, 183
"Goethe and Democracy" (Mann), 147, 148n
Goethe Society, 170
Gogoi, *see* Borgese, Angelica
Goldman, Hetty, 127, 129n
Greenberg, Martin, 180n
Green Henry (Keller), 124n
Gregorius auf dem Steine, 144, 145n
Gregorius story, see *Holy Sinner, The*
Grimmelshausen, H. J. C. von, 140n
Groth, Rudolf, 130
Grüne Heinrich, Der (Keller), 124n
Grzesinsky, Albert Carl, 59, 61n
Gundolf, Friedrich, vii, 5, 7n

Halifax, Edward Frederick, Earl of, 54

[193]

An Exceptional Friendship

Designed by R. E. Rosenbaum.
Composed by Cayuga Press, Inc.,
in 11 point Intertype Baskerville, 2 points leaded,
with display lines in Monotype Baskerville.
Printed letterpress from type by Cayuga Press
on Warren's No. 66 text, 50 pound basis,
with the Cornell University Press watermark.
Bound by Vail-Ballou Press
in Columbia book cloth
and stamped in All Purpose foil.